Managing Human Resources in Retail Organizations

The Advances in Retailing Series

The Institute of Retail Management (IRM) was established to advance the understanding and practice of retailing by serving as a bridge between the academic community and industry. Two of the principal avenues the IRM uses to achieve this goal are conferences focusing on the latest ideas and research, and publications, including the *Journal of Retailing* and conference proceedings. Thus, the IRM's two most important audiences are academic scholars and practitioners in retailing-related fields.

The Advances in Retailing Series is a point of intersection for the IRM's conference and publication programs. Initiated with valuable input from both retailers and academics, the series presents an enduring collection of up-to-date studies of problems and issues in retailing theory and practice. It is intended to respond to a variety of pervasive needs by: presenting timely assessments of new developments in the field, bringing fresh perspectives from other industries to critical issues in retailing, stimulating further research on challenging issues raised at conferences, and fostering productive communication and cooperation between retailing executives and academic researchers.

We believe that, as a whole, this series effectively addresses these and other needs. We invite comments and suggestions from our readers on how it can best fulfill its purpose.

The books in the Advances in Retailing Series are:

Personal Selling: Theory, Research, and Practice
Edited by Jacob Jacoby and C. Samuel Craig

Managing Human Resources in Retail Organizations
Edited by Arthur P. Brief

Consumer Perception of Merchandise and Store Quality
Edited by Jacob Jacoby and Jerry C. Olson

The Service Encounter
Edited by John A. Czepiel, Michael R. Solomon, and Carol Suprenant

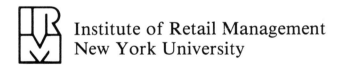 Institute of Retail Management
New York University

Managing Human Resources in Retail Organizations

Edited by
Arthur P. Brief
New York University

LexingtonBooks
D.C. Heath and Company
Lexington, Massachusetts
Toronto

Library of Congress Cataloging in Publication Data
Main entry under title:

Managing human resources in retail organizations.

    1. Retail trade—Personnel management—Addresses,
essays, lectures. 2. Personnel management—Addresses,
essays, lectures. I. Brief, Arthur P., 1946–
HF5429.26.M36 1984   658.8′7′00683   83–49496
ISBN 0–669–08149–3 (alk. paper)

Copyright © 1984 by D.C. Heath and Company

Published simultaneously in Canada

Printed in the United States of America

International Standard Book Number: 0–669–08149–3

Library of Congress Catalog Card Number: 83–49496

To Laura—the twinkle in my eye

Contents

Introduction

In 1983, the Institute of Retail Management of New York University's Schools of Business and Korn/Ferry International, Inc., jointly sponsored a conference on managing human resources in retail organizations. In part, the intent of the conference was to stimulate industry executives to apply more aggressively the knowledge generated by academic researchers to solving the problems of managing people in retail organizations. The retailers attending were introduced to this knowledge base by four distinguished researchers as well as by myself, who along with Howard Falberg of Associated Dry Goods, Inc., served as conference co-chairperson.

This edited collection consists of executive summaries of the researchers' presentations and more comprehensive surveys of the research they reviewed. In addition, the book concludes with a piece which has the purpose of specifying a personnel research agenda reflective of the needs of retailing executives.

Substantively, four broad areas of research are reviewed. First, Dr. Edwin Locke of the University of Maryland discusses the efficacy of goal-setting programs as means of boosting employee performance. Second, the literature on performance appraisal is reviewed by Dr. Richard Klimoski of Ohio State University. Third, Dr. Randall Schuler of New York University addresses various approaches to stress management. Finally, Dr. Benjamin Schneider of the University of Maryland provides an overview of techniques for improving employee productivity. Collectively, these four substantive areas are seen as focusing on issues key to the successful management of human resources in retail organizations. Thus, the intent of offering a review of them in this single source is to provide a retailing audience with the knowledge base required to pursue aggressively the enhancement of human resources management practices within the industry. With the addition of the concluding chapter on a personnel research agenda, it is anticipated that the book will not only provide a foundation for current practice but also suggest the types of applied research findings required in the decades ahead.

1

Goal Setting—
A Motivational
Technique That Works

Gary P. Latham and
Edwin A. Locke

The problem of how to motivate employees has puzzled and frustrated managers for generations. One reason the problem has seemed difficult, if not mysterious, is that motivation ultimately comes from within the individual and therefore cannot be observed directly. Moreover, most managers are not in a position to change an employee's basic personality structure. The best they can do is try to use incentives to direct the energies of their employees toward organizational objectives.

Money is obviously the primary incentive, since without it few if any employees would come to work. But money alone is not always enough to motivate high performance. Other incentives, such as participation in decision making, job enrichment, behavior modification, and organizational development, have been tried with varying degrees of success. A large number of research studies have shown, however, that one very straightforward technique—goal setting—is probably not only more effective than alternative methods, but may be the major mechanism by which these other incentives affect motivation. For example, a recent experiment on job enrichment demonstrated that unless employees in enriched jobs set higher, more specific goals than do those with unenriched jobs, job enrichment has absolutely no effect on productivity. Even money has been found most effective as a motivator when the bonuses offered are made contingent on attaining specific objectives.

The Goal-Setting Concept

The idea of assigning employees a specific amount of work to be accomplished—a specific task, a quota, a performance standard, an objective, or a deadline—is not new. The task concept, along with time and motion study and incentive pay, was the cornerstone of scientific management, founded by Frederick W. Taylor more than seventy years ago. He used his system to increase the productivity of blue-collar workers. About twenty years ago the idea of goal setting reappeared under a new name, management by objectives, but this technique was designed for managers.

In a fourteen-year program of research, we have found that goal setting does not necessarily have to be part of a wider management system to motivate performance effectively. It can be used as a technique in its own right.

Laboratory and Field Research

Our research program began in the laboratory. In a series of experiments, individuals were assigned different types of goals on a variety of simple tasks—addition, brainstorming, assembling toys. Repeatedly it was found that those assigned hard goals performed better than did people assigned moderately difficult or easy goals. Furthermore, individuals who had specific, challenging goals outperformed those who were given such vague goals as to "do your best." Finally, we observed that pay and performance feedback led to improved performance only when these incentives led the individual to set higher goals.

While results were quite consistent in the laboratory, there was no proof that they could be applied to actual work settings. Fortunately, just as Locke published a summary of the laboratory studies in 1968, Latham began a separate series of experiments in the wood products industry that demonstrated the practical significance of these findings. The field studies did not start out as a validity test of a laboratory theory, but rather as a response to a practical problem.

In 1968, six sponsors of the American Pulpwood Association became concerned about increasing the productivity of independent loggers in the South. These loggers were entrepreneurs on whom the multimillion-dollar companies are largely dependent for their raw material. The problem was twofold. First, these entrepreneurs did not work for a single company; they worked for themselves. Thus they were free to (and often did) work two days one week, four days a second week, five half-days a third week, or whatever schedule they preferred. In short, these workers could be classified as marginal from the standpoint of their productivity and attendance, which were considered highly unsatisfactory by conventional company standards. Second, the major approach taken to alleviate this problem had been to develop equipment that would make the industry less dependent on this type of worker. A limitation of this approach was that many of the logging supervisors were unable to obtain the financing necessary to purchase a small tractor, let alone a rubber-tired skidder.

Consequently, we designed a survey that would help managers determine "what makes these people tick." The survey was conducted orally in the field with 292 logging supervisors. Complex statistical analyses of the data identified three basic types of supervisor. One type stayed on the job with their men, gave them instructions and explanations, provided them with training, read the trade magazines, and had little difficulty financing the equipment they needed. Still, the productivity of their units was at best mediocre.

The operation of the second group of supervisors was slightly less mechanized. These supervisors provided little training for their workforce. They simply drove their employees to the woods, gave them a specific production goal to attain for the day or week, left them alone in the woods unsupervised, and returned at night to take them home. Labor turnover was high and productivity was again average.

The operation of the third group of supervisors was relatively unmechanized. These leaders stayed on the job with their men, provided training, gave instructions and explanations, and in addition, set a specific production goal for the day or week. Not only was the crew's productivity high, but their injury rate was well below average.

Two conclusions were discussed with the managers of the companies sponsoring this study. First, mechanization alone will not increase the productivity of logging crews. Just as the average taxpayer would probably commit more mathematical errors if he were to try to use a computer to complete his income tax return, the average logger misuses, and frequently abuses, the equipment he purchases (for example, drives a skidder with two flat tires, doesn't change the oil filter). This increases not only the logger's downtime, but also his costs which, in turn, can force him out of business. The second conclusion of the survey was that setting a specific production goal combined with supervisory presence to ensure goal commitment will bring about a significant increase in productivity.

These conclusions were greeted with the standard, but valid, cliché, "Statistics don't prove causation." And our comments regarding the value of machinery were especially irritating to these managers, many of whom had received degrees in engineering. So one of the companies decided to replicate the survey in order to check our findings.

The company's study placed each of 892 independent logging supervisors who sold wood to the company into one of three categories of supervisory styles our survey had identified—namely, (1) stays on the job but does not set specific production goals; (2) sets specific production goals but does not stay on the job; and (3) stays on the job and sets specific production goals. Once again, goal setting, in combination with the on-site presence of a supervisor, was shown to be the key to improved productivity.

Testing for the Hawthorne Effect

Management may have been unfamiliar with different theories of motivation, but it was fully aware of one label—the Hawthorne effect. Managers in these wood products companies remained unconvinced that anything so simple as staying on the job with the men and setting a specific production goal could have an appreciable effect on productivity. They pointed out that the results simply reflected the positive effects any supervisor would have on the work unit after giving his crew attention. And they were unimpressed by the laboratory experiments we cited—experiments showing that individuals who have a specific goal solve more arithmetic problems or assemble more tinker toys than do people who are told to "do your best." Skepticism prevailed.

But the country's economic picture made it critical to continue the study of inexpensive techniques to improve employee motivation and productivity. We were granted permission to run one more project to test the effectiveness of goal setting.

Twenty independent logging crews who were all but identical in size, mechanization level, terrain on which they worked, productivity, and attendance were located. The logging supervisors of these crews were in the habit of staying on the job with their men, but they did not set production goals. Half the crews were randomly selected to receive training in goal setting; the remaining crews served as a control group.

The logging supervisors who were to set goals were told that we had found a way to increase productivity at no financial expense to anyone. We gave the ten supervisors in the training group production tables developed through time-and-motion studies by the company's engineers. These tables made it possible to determine how much wood should be harvested in a given number of manhours. They were asked to use these tables as a guide in determining a specific production goal to assign their employees. In addition, each sawhand was given a tallymeter (counter) that he could wear on his belt. The sawhand was asked to punch the counter each time he felled a tree. Finally, permission was requested to measure the crew's performance on a weekly basis.

The ten supervisors in the control group—those who were not

asked to set production goals—were told that the researchers were interested in learning the extent to which productivity is affected by absenteeism and injuries. They were urged to "do your best" to maximize the crew's productivity and attendance and to minimize injuries. It was explained that the data might be useful in finding ways to increase productivity at little or no cost to the wood harvester.

To control for the Hawthorne effect, we made an equal number of visits to the control group and the training group. Performance was measured for twelve weeks. During this time, the productivity of the goal-setting group was significantly higher than that of the control group. Moreover, absenteeism was significantly lower in the groups that set goals than in the groups who were simply urged to do their best. Injury and turnover rates were low in both groups.

Why should anything so simple and inexpensive as goal setting influence the work of these employees so significantly? Anecdotal evidence from conversations with both the loggers and the company foresters who visited them suggested several reasons.

Harvesting timber can be a monotonous, tiring job with little or no meaning for most workers. Introducing a goal that is difficult, but attainable, increases the challenge of the job. In addition, a specific goal makes it clear to the worker what it is he is expected to do. Goal feedback via the tallymeter and weekly recordkeeping provide the worker with a sense of achievement, recognition, and accomplishment. He can see how well he is doing now as against his past performance and, in some cases, how well he is doing in comparison with others. Thus the worker not only may expend greater effort, but may also devise better or more creative tactics for attaining the goal than those he previously used.

New Applications

Management was finally convinced that goal setting was an effective motivational technique for increasing the productivity of the independent woods worker in the South. The issue now raised by the management of another wood products company was whether the procedure could be used in the West with company logging operations in which the employees were unionized and paid by the hour. The previous study had involved employees on a piece-rate system, which was the practice in the South.

The immediate problem confronting this company involved the loading of logging trucks. If the trucks were underloaded, the company lost money. If the trucks were overloaded, however, the driver could be fined by the Highway Department and could ultimately lose his job. The drivers opted for underloading the trucks.

For three months management tried to solve this problem by urging the drivers to try harder to fill the truck to its legal net weight, and by developing weighing scales that could be attached to the truck. But this approach did not prove cost effective, because the scales continually broke down when subjected to the rough terrain on which the trucks traveled. Consequently, the drivers reverted to their former practice of underloading. For the three months in which the problem was under study the trucks were seldom loaded in excess of 58 to 63 percent of capacity.

At the end of the three-month period, the results of the previous goal-setting experiments were explained to the union. They were told three things—that the company would like to set a specific net weight goal for the drivers, that no monetary reward or fringe benefits other than verbal praise could be expected for improved performance, and that no one would be criticized for failing to attain the goal. Once again, the idea that simply setting a specific goal would solve a production problem seemed too incredible to be taken seriously by the union. However, they reached an agreement that a difficult, but attainable, goal of 94 percent of the truck's legal net weight would be assigned to the drivers, provided that no one could be reprimanded for failing to attain the goal. This latter point was emphasized to the company foremen in particular.

Within the first month, performance increased to 80 percent of the truck's net weight. After the second month, however, performance decreased to 70 percent. Interviews with the drivers indicated that they were testing management's statement that no punitive steps would be taken against them if their performance suddenly dropped. Fortunately for all concerned, no such steps were taken by the foremen, and performance exceeded 90 percent of the truck's capacity after the third month. Their performance has remained at this level to this day, seven years later.

The results over the nine-month period during which this study was conducted saved the company $250,000. This figure, determined by the company's accountants, is based on the cost of additional trucks that would have been required to deliver the same quantity of logs to the mill if goal setting had not been implemented. The dollars-saved figure is even higher when you factor in the cost of the additional diesel fuel that would have been consumed and the expenses incurred in recruiting and hiring the additional truck drivers.

Why could this procedure work without the union's demanding an increase in hourly wages? First, the drivers did not feel that they were really doing anything differently. This, of course, was not true. As a result of goal setting, the men began to record their truck weight in a pocket notebook, and they found themselves bragging about their accomplishments to their peers. Second, they viewed goal setting as a challenging game: "It was great to beat the other guy."

Competition was a crucial factor in bringing about goal acceptance and commitment in this study. However, we can reject the hypothesis that improved performance resulted solely from competition, because no special prizes or formal recognition programs were provided for those who came closest to, or exceeded, the goal. No effort was made by the company to single out one "winner." More important, the opportunity for competition among drivers had existed before goal setting was instituted; after all, each driver knew his own truck's weight, and the truck weight of each of the thirty-six other drivers every time he hauled wood into the yard. In short, competition affected productivity only in the sense that it led to the acceptance of, and commitment to, the goal. It was the setting of the goal itself and the working toward it that brought about increased performance and decreased costs.

Participative Goal Setting

The inevitable question always raised by management was raised here: "We know goal setting works. How can we make it work better?" Was there one best method for setting goals? Evidence for a "one best way" approach was cited by several managers, but it was finally concluded that different approaches would work best under different circumstances.

It was hypothesized that the woods workers in the South, who had little or no education, would work better with assigned goals, while the educated workers in the West would achieve higher productivity if they were allowed to help set the goals themselves. Why the focus on education? Many of the uneducated workers in the South could be classified as culturally disadvantaged. Such persons often lack self-confidence, have a poor sense of time, and are not very competitive. The cycle of skill mastery, which in turn guarantees skill levels high enough to prevent discouragement, doesn't apply to these employees. If, for example, these people were allowed to participate in goal setting, the goals might be too difficult or they might be too easy. On the other hand, participation for the educated worker was considered critical in effecting maximum goal acceptance. Since these conclusions appeared logical, management initially decided that no research was necessary. This decision led to hours of further discussion.

The same questions were raised again and again by the researchers. What if the logic were wrong? Can we afford to implement these decisions without evaluating them systematically? Would we implement decisions regarding a new approach to tree planting without first testing it? Do we care more about trees than we do about people? Finally, permission was granted to conduct an experiment.

Logging crews were randomly appointed to either participative goal setting, assigned (nonparticipative) goal setting, or a do-your-best condition. The results were startling. The uneducated crews, consisting primarily of black employees who participated in goal setting, set significantly higher goals and attained them more often than did those whose goals were assigned by the supervisor. Not surprisingly, their performance was higher. Crews with assigned goals performed no better than did those who were urged to do their best to improve their productivity. The performance of white, educationally advantaged workers was higher with assigned rather than participatively set goals, although the difference was not statistically significant. These results were precisely the opposite of what had been predicted.

Another study comparing participative and assigned goals was conducted with typists. The results supported findings obtained by researchers at General Electric years before. It did not matter so much *how* the goal was set. What mattered was *that* a goal was set. The study demonstrated that both assigned and participatively set goals led to substantial improvements in typing speed. The process by which these gains occurred, however, differed in the two groups.

In the participative group, employees insisted on setting very high goals regardless of whether they had attained their goal the previous week. Nevertheless, their productivity improved—an outcome consistent with the theory that high goals lead to high performance.

In the assigned-goal group, supervisors were highly supportive of employees. No criticism was given for failure to attain the goals. Instead, the supervisor lowered the goal after failure so that the employee would be certain to attain it. The goal was then raised gradually each week until the supervisor felt the employee was achieving his or her potential. The result? Feelings of accomplishment and achievement on the part of the worker and improved productivity for the company.

These basic findings were replicated in a subsequent study of engineers and scientists. Participative goal setting was superior to assigned goal setting only to the degree that it led to the setting of higher goals. Both participative and assigned-goal groups outperformed groups that were simply told to "do your best."

An additional experiment was conducted to validate the conclusion that participation in goal setting may be important only to the extent that it leads to the setting of difficult goals. It was performed in a laboratory setting in which the task was to brainstorm uses for wood. One group was asked to "do your best" to think of as many ideas as possible. A second group took part in deciding, with the experimenter, the specific number of ideas each person would generate. These goals were, in turn, assigned to individuals in a third group. In this way, goal difficulty was held constant between the assigned-goal and participative groups. Again, it was found that specific, difficult goals—whether assigned or set through participation—led to higher performance than did an abstract or generalized goal such as "do your best." And, when goal difficulty was held constant, there was no significant difference in the performance of those with assigned as compared with participatively set goals.

These results demonstrate that goal setting in industry works just as it does in the laboratory. Specific, challenging goals lead to better performance than do easy or vague goals, and feedback motivates higher performance only when it leads to the setting of higher goals.

It is important to note that participation is not only a motivational tool. When a manager has competent subordinates, participation is also a useful device for increasing the manager's knowledge and thereby improving decision quality. It can lead to better decisions through input from subordinates.

A representative sample of the results of field studies of goal setting conducted by Latham and others is shown in table 1–1. Each of these ten studies compared the performance of employees given specific challenging goals with those given "do best" or no goals. Note that goal setting has been successful across a wide variety of jobs and industries. The effects of goal setting have been recorded for as long as seven years after the onset of the program, although the results of most studies have been followed up for only a few weeks or months. The median improvement in performance in the ten studies shown in table 1–1 was 17 percent.

A Critical Incidents Survey

To explore further the importance of goal setting in the work setting, Dr. Frank White conducted another study in two plants of a high-technology, multinational corporation on the East Coast. Seventy-one engineers, fifty managers, and thirty-one clerks were asked to describe a specific instance when they were especially productive and a specific instance when they were especially unproductive on their present jobs. Responses were classified according to a reliable coding scheme. Of

Table 1–1
Representative Field Studies of Goal Setting

Researcher(s)	Task	Duration of Study or of Significant Effects	Percent of Change in Performance [a]
Blumenfeld & Leidy	Servicing soft drink coolers	Unspecified	+27
Dockstader	Keypunching	3 mos.	+27
Ivancevich	Skilled technical jobs	9 mos.	+15
Ivancevich	Sales	9 mos.	+24
Kim and Hamner	5 telephone service jobs	3 mos.	+13
Latham and Baldes	Loading trucks	9 mos.[b]	+26
Latham and Yukl	Logging	2 mos.	+18
Latham and Yukl	Typing	5 weeks	+11
Migliore	Mass production	2 years	+16
Umstot, Bell, and Mitchell	Coding land parcels	1–2 days[c]	+16

[a]Percentage changes were obtained by subtracting pre-goal-setting performance from post-goal-setting performance and dividing by pre-goal-setting performance. Different experimental groups were combined where appropriate. If a control group was available, the percentage figure represents the difference of the percentage changes between the experimental and control groups. If multiple performance measures were used, the median improvement on all measures was used. The authors would like to thank Dena Feren and Vicki McCaleb for performing these calculations.
[b]Performance has remained high for seven years.
[c]Simulated organization.

primary interest here are the external events perceived by employees as being responsible for the high-productivity and low-productivity incidents. The results are shown in table 1–2.

The first set of events—pursuing a specific goal, having a large amount of work, working under a deadline, or having an uninterrupted routine—accounted for more than half the high-productivity events. Similarly, the converse of these—goal blockage, having a small amount of work, lacking a deadline, and suffering work interruptions—accounted for nearly 60 percent of the low-productivity events. Note that the first set of our categories are all relevant to goal setting and the second set to a lack of goals or goal blockage. The goal category itself—that of pursuing an attainable goal or goal blockage—was the one most frequently used to describe high- and low-productivity incidents.

The next four categories, which are more pertinent to Frederick Herzberg's motivator-hygiene theory—task interest, responsibility, promotion, and recognition—are less important, accounting for 36.8

Table 1–2
Events Perceived as Causing High and Low Productivity[a]

Event	Percent of Times Event Caused	
	High Productivity	Low Productivity
Goal pursuit/Goal blockage	17.1	23.0
Large amount of work/Small amount of work	12.5	19.0
Deadline or schedule/No deadline	15.1	3.3
Smooth work routine/Interrupted routine	5.9	14.5
Total	50.6	59.8
Interesting task/Uninteresting task	17.1	11.2
Increased responsibility/Decreased responsibility	13.8	4.6
Anticipated promotion/Promotion denied	1.3	0.7
Verbal recognition/Criticism	4.6	2.6
Total	36.8	19.1
Pleasant personal relationships/ Unpleasant personal relationships	10.5	9.9
Anticipated pay increase/Pay increase denied	1.3	1.3
Pleasant working conditions/ Unpleasant working conditions	0.7	0.7
Other (miscellaneous)	—	9.3

[a]$N = 152$ in this study by Frank White.

percent of the high-productivity incidents (the opposite of these four categories accounted for 19.1 percent of the lows). The remaining categories were even less important.

Employees were also asked to identify the responsible agent behind the events that had led to high and low productivity. In both cases, the employees themselves, their immediate supervisors, and the organization were the agents most frequently mentioned.

The concept of goal setting is a very simple one. Interestingly, however, we have gotten two contradictory types of reaction when the idea was introduced to managers. Some claimed it was so simple and self-evident that everyone, including themselves, already used it. This, we have found, is not true. Time after time we have gotten the following response from subordinates after goal setting was introduced: "This is the first time I knew what my supervisor expected of me on this job." Conversely, other managers have argued that the idea would not work, precisely *because* it is so simple (implying that something more radical and complex was needed). Again, results proved them wrong.

But these successes should not mislead managers into thinking that goal setting can be used without careful planning and forethought. Research and experience suggest that the best results are obtained when the following steps are followed:

Setting the Goal. The goal set should have two main characteristics. First, it should be specific rather than vague: "Increase sales by 10 percent" rather than "Try to improve sales." Whenever possible, there should be a time limit for goal accomplishment: "Cut costs by 3 percent in the next six months."

Second, the goal should be challenging yet reachable. If accepted, difficult goals lead to better performance than do easy goals. In contrast, if the goals are perceived as unreachable, employees will not accept them. Nor will employees get a sense of achievement from pursuing goals that are never attained. Employees with low self-confidence or ability should be given more easily attainable goals than those with high self-confidence and ability.

There are at least five possible sources of input, aside from the individual's self-confidence and ability, that can be used to determine the particular goal to set for a given individual.

The scientific management approach pioneered by Frederick W. Taylor uses time and motion study to determine a fair day's work. This is probably the most objective technique available, but it can be used only where the task is reasonably repetitive and standardized. Another drawback is that this method often leads to employee resistance, especially in cases where the new standard is substantially higher than previous performance and where rate changes are made frequently.

More readily accepted, although less scientific than time and motion study, are standards based on the average past performance of employees. This method was used successfully in some of our field studies. Most employees consider this approach fair but, naturally, in cases where past performance is far below capacity, beating that standard will be extremely easy.

Since goal setting is sometimes simply a matter of judgment, another technique we have used is to allow the goal to be set jointly by supervisor and subordinate. The participative approach may be less scientific than time and motion study, but it does lead to ready acceptance by both employee and immediate superior in addition to promoting role clarity.

External constraints often affect goal setting, especially among managers. For example, the goal to produce an item at a certain price may be dictated by the actions of competitors, and deadlines may be imposed externally in line with contract agreements. Legal regulations, such as attaining a certain reduction in pollution levels by a certain date, may affect goal setting as well. In these cases, setting the goal is not so much the problem as is figuring out a method of reaching it.

Finally, organizational goals set by the board of directors or upper management will influence the goals set by employees at lower levels. This is the essence of the MBO process.

Another issue that needs to be considered when setting goals is whether they should be designed for individuals or for groups. Rensis Likert and a number of other human relations experts argue for group goal setting on grounds that it promotes cooperation and team spirit. But one could argue that individual goals better promote individual responsibility and make it easier to appraise individual performance. The degree of task interdependence involved would also be a factor to consider.

Obtaining Goal Commitment. If goal setting is to work, then the manager must ensure that subordinates will accept and remain committed to the goals. Simple instruction backed by positive support and an absence of threats or intimidation were enough to ensure goal acceptance in most of our studies. Subordinates must perceive the goals as fair and reasonable and they must trust management, for if they perceive the goals as no more than a means of exploitation, they will be likely to reject the goals.

It may seem surprising that goal acceptance was achieved so readily in the field studies. Remember, however, that in all cases the employees were receiving wages or a salary (although these were not necessarily directly contingent on goal attainment). Pay in combination with the supervisor's benevolent authority and supportiveness were sufficient to bring about goal acceptance. Recent research indicates that whether goals are assigned or set participatively, supportiveness on the part of the immediate superior is critical. A supportive manager or supervisor does not use goals to threaten subordinates, but rather to clarify what is expected of them. His or her role is that of a helper and goal facilitator.

As noted earlier, the employee gets a feeling of pride and satisfaction from the experience of reaching a challenging but fair performance goal. Success in reaching a goal also tends to reinforce acceptance of future goals. Once goal setting is introduced, informal competition frequently arises among the employees. This further reinforces commitment and may lead employees to raise the goals spontaneously. A word of caution here, however: We do not recommend setting up formal competition, as this may lead employees to place individual goals ahead of company goals. The emphasis should be on accomplishing the task, getting the job done, not "beating" the other person.

When employees resist assigned goals, they generally do so for one of two reasons. First, they may think they are incapable of reaching the goal because they lack confidence, ability, knowledge, and the like. Second, they may not see any personal benefit—either in terms of personal pride or in terms of external rewards like money, promotion, recognition—in reaching assigned goals.

There are various methods of overcoming employee resistance to goals. One possibility is more training designed to raise the employee's level of skill and self-confidence. Allowing the subordinate to participate in setting the goal—deciding on the goal level—is another method. This was found most effective among uneducated and minority group employees, perhaps because it gave them a feeling of control over their fate. Offering monetary bonuses or other rewards (recognition, time off) for reaching goals may also help.

The last two methods may be especially useful where there is a history of labor-management conflict and where employees have become accustomed to a lower level of effort than currently considered acceptable. Group incentives may also encourage goal acceptance, especially where there is a group goal, or when considerable cooperation is required.

Providing Support Elements. A third step to take when introducing goal setting is to ensure the availability of necessary support elements. That is, the employee must be given adequate resources—money, equipment, time, help—as well as the freedom to utilize them in attaining goals, and company policies must not work to block goal attainment.

Before turning an employee loose with these resources, however, it's wise to do a quick check on whether conditions are optimum for reaching the goal set. First, the supervisor must make sure that the employee has sufficient ability and knowledge to be able to reach the goal. Motivation without knowledge is useless. This, of course, puts a premium on proper selection and training and requires that the supervisor know the capabilities of subordinates when goals are assigned. Asking an employee to formulate an action plan for reaching the goal, as in MBO, is very useful, as it will indicate any knowledge deficiencies.

Second, the supervisor must ensure that the employee is provided with precise feedback so that he will know to what degree he is reaching or falling short of his goal and can thereupon adjust his level of effort or strategy accordingly. Recent research indicates that, while feedback is not a sufficient condition for improved performance, it is a necessary condition. A useful way to present periodic feedback is through the use of charts or graphs that plot performance over time.

Elements involved in taking the three steps described are shown in figure 1–1, which illustrates in outline form our model of goal setting.

Conclusion

We believe that goal setting is a simple, straightforward, and highly effective technique for motivating employee performance. It is a basic technique, a method on which most other methods depend for their motivational effectiveness. The currently popular technique of behavior modification, for example, is mainly goal setting plus feedback, dressed up in academic terminology.

However, goal setting is no panacea. It will not compensate for underpayment of employees or for poor management. Used incorrectly, goal setting may cause rather than solve problems. If, for example, the goals set are unfair, arbitrary, or unreachable, dissatisfaction and poor performance may result. If difficult goals are set without proper quality controls, quantity may be achieved at the expense of quality. If pressure for immediate results is exerted without regard to how they are attained, short-term improvement may occur at the expense of long-run profits. That is, such pressure often triggers the use of expedient and ultimately costly methods—such as dishonesty, high-pressure tactics, postponing of maintenance expenses, and so on—to attain immediate results. Furthermore, performance goals are more easily set in some areas than in others. It is all too easy, for example, to concentrate on setting readily measured production goals and ignore employee development goals. Like any other management tool, goal setting works only when combined with good managerial judgment.

Selected Bibliography

A summary of the early (mainly laboratory) research on goal setting may be found in E.A. Locke's "Toward a Theory of Task Motivation and Incentives" (*Organization Behavior and Human Performance,* May 1968). More recent reviews that include some of the early field studies are reported by G.P. Latham and G.A. Yukl's "Review of Research on the Application of Goal Setting in Organizations" (*Academy of Management Journal,* December 1975) and in R.M. Steers and L.W. Porter's "The Role of Task–Goal Attributes in Employee Performance" (*Psychological Bulletin,* July 1974).
An excellent historical discussion of management by objectives, in-

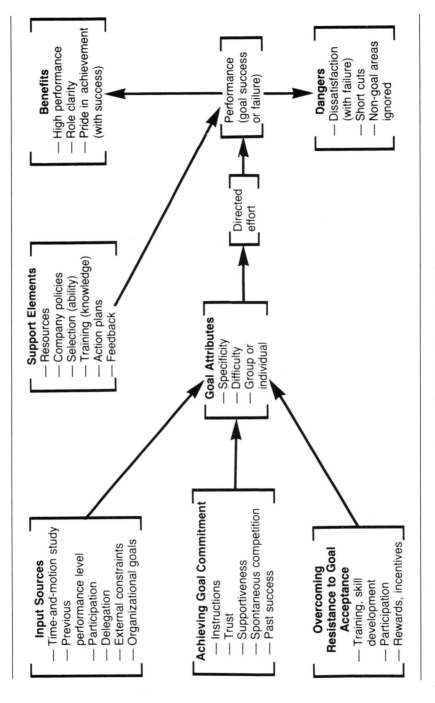

Figure 1–1. Goal-Setting Model

cluding its relationship to goal-setting research, can be found in G.S. Odiorne's "MBO: A Backward Glance" (*Business Horizons*, October 1978).

A thorough review of the literature on participation, including the relationship of participation and goal setting, can be found in a chapter by E.A. Locke and D.M. Schweiger, "Participation in Decision-Making: One More Look," in B.M. Staw's edited work, *Research in Organizational Behavior* (Vol. 1, Greenwich, JAI Press, 1979). General Electric's famous research on the effect of participation in the appraisal interview is summarized in H.H. Meyer, E. Kay, and J.R.P. French, Jr.'s "Split Roles in Performance Appraisal" (*Harvard Business Review*, January–February 1965).

The relationship of goal setting to knowledge of results is discussed in E.A. Locke, N. Cartledge, and J. Koeppel's "Motivational Effects of Knowledge of Results: A Goal Setting Phenomenon?" (*Psychological Bulletin*, December 1968) and L.J. Becker's "Joint Effect of Feedback and Goal Setting on Performance: A Field Study of Residential Energy Conservation" (*Journal of Applied Psychology*, August 1978). Finally, the role of goal setting in virtually all theories of work motivation is documented in E.A. Locke's "The Ubiquity of the Technique of Goal Setting in Theories of and Approaches to Employee Motivation" (*Academy of Management Review*, July 1978).

2

Goal Setting and Task Performance: 1969–1980

Edwin A. Locke,
Karyll N. Shaw, Lise M. Saari,
and *Gary P. Latham*

In this chapter we summarize research relating to (1) the effects of setting various types of goals or objectives on task performance and (2) the factors (other than the goals themselves) that influence the effectiveness of goal setting.

All-encompassing theories of motivation based on such concepts as instinct, drive, and conditioning have not succeeded in explaining human action. Such theories have been gradually replaced by more modest and limited approaches to motivation. These approaches do not presume to explain all motivational phenomena; their domains are more restricted. The study of goal setting is one such limited approach. The concept of goal setting falls within the broad domain of cognitive psychology and is consistent with recent trends such as cognitive behavior modification (Meichenbaum, 1977). The present interest of researchers in goal setting has two sources, one academic and the other organizational. The academic source extends back in time from Ryan (1970) and G. Miller, Galanter, and Pribram (1960), through Lewin, to the Wurzburg School and the associated concepts of intention, task, set, and level of aspiration (see Ryan, 1970, for a summary). The organizational source is traced from Management by Objectives programs, now widely used in industry (see Odiorne, 1978, for a summary), back to the Scientific Management movement founded by Frederick W. Taylor (1911/1967). These two strains of thought converge in the more recent work of Locke (1968), Latham (Latham and Yukl, 1975b), and others who have studied the effects of goal setting on task performance. Goal setting is also an important component of

Preparation of this manuscript was supported by Office of Naval Research Contract N00014-79-C-0680.

social learning theory (Bandura, 1977), which has become increasingly influential in recent years. Even the literature on organizational behavior modification can be interpreted largely within a goal-setting framework (Locke, 1977).

Research on goal setting is proliferating so rapidly that recent reviews (Latham and Yukl, 1975b; Locke,1968; Steers and Porter, 1974) are now outdated. To provide a longer-term perspective than just the last six years, our review includes research published since 1968. Studies that are explicitly clinical and social–psychological in nature are not included (for a detailed review of the latter, see Fishbein and Ajzen, 1975).

The Concept of Goal Setting

A goal is what an individual is trying to accomplish; it is the object or aim of an action. The concept is similar in meaning to the concepts of purpose and intent (Locke, 1969). Other frequently used concepts that are also similar in meaning to that of goal include performance standard (a measuring rod for evaluating performance), quota (a minimum amount of work or production), work norm (a standard of acceptable behavior defined by a work group), task (a piece of work to be accomplished), objective (the ultimate aim of an action or series of actions), deadline (a time limit for completing a task), and budget (a spending goal or limit).

Earlier attempts by behaviorists to reduce concepts like goal and purpose to physical events have been strongly criticized (for instance, see Locke, 1969, 1972). Goal setting might be called "stimulus control" by a modern behaviorist, but the key question then becomes, What is the stimulus? If it is only an assigned goal (an environmental event), then the importance of goal acceptance is ignored; an assigned goal that is rejected can hardly regulate performance. If goal acceptance is considered relevant, then the regulating stimulus must be a mental event—ultimately the individual's goal. The environment, of course, can influence goal setting as well as goal acceptance, an issue that is dealt with in some of the recent research.

The basic assumption of goal-setting research is that goals are immediate regulators of human action. However, no one-to-one correspondence between goals and action is assumed because people may make errors, lack the ability to attain their objectives (Locke, 1968), or have subconscious conflicts or premises that subvert their conscious goals. The precise degree of association between goals and action is an empirical question that is dealt with in the reserach we review here.

We also examine the mechanisms by which goals affect action, the effects of feedback, participation, and money on goal-setting effectiveness, the role of individual differences, and the determinants of goal commitment.

Goal-Setting Attributes[1]

Mental processes have two major attributes, content and intensity (Rand, 1967). The content of a goal is the object or result being sought. The main dimensions of goal content that have been studied so far are specificity or clarity (the degree of quantitative precision with which the aim is specified) and difficulty (the degree of proficiency or level of performance sought). The terms *task difficulty* and *goal difficulty* are often used interchangeably, but a distinction between them can be made.

A task is a piece of work to be accomplished. A difficult task is one that is hard to do. A task can be hard because it is complex, that is, requires a high level of skill and knowledge. For example, writing a book on physics is a harder task than writing a thank-you note. A task can also be hard because it requires a great deal of effort: digging the foundation for a pool takes more effort than digging a hole to plant a flower seed.

Since a goal is the object or aim of an action, it is possible for the completion of a task to be a goal. However, in most goal-setting studies, the term *goal* refers to attaining a specific standard of proficiency on a task, usually within a specified time limit. For example, two individuals are given the same task (for instance, simple addition), but one is asked to complete a large number of problems within 30 minutes, and the other, a small number. The harder goal would be achieved by expending greater effort and attention than would be expended to achieve the easy goal. Harder goals, like harder tasks, also can require more knowledge and skill than easier goals (for instance, winning a chess tournament vs. coming in next to last). To summarize the distinction between the terms, goal difficulty specifies a certain level of task proficiency measured against a standard, whereas task difficulty refers simply to the nature of the work to be accomplished.

Although greater task difficulty should lead to greater effort (Kahneman, 1973; Kaplan and Rothkopf, 1974; Shapira[2]), the relation of task difficulty to performance is problematic. If more work is translated into a goal to get more done, task difficulty may be positively related to performance (Sales, 1970). On the other hand, if harder tasks require more ability or knowledge, most people will, at least initially, perform less well on them, even if they try harder, than they would on easier tasks (see note 2).

An experiment by Campbell and Ilgen (1976) demonstrated that the distinction between task and goal difficulty has practical utility. Thney manipulated both dimensions independently. On chess problems difficult goals led to better performance than easy goals; training subjects on hard problems (tasks) led at first to poorer performance but later to better performance than training subjects on easier problems (tasks). Presumably the harder goals led to greater effort than the easier goals, and training on the harder chess problems led to the acquisition of more skill and knowledge than training on easier ones.

Although there has been extensive research on the effects of goal specificity and difficulty on performance, little attention has been paid to two other dimensions of goal content: goal complexity (the number and interrelation of the results aimed for) and goal conflict (the degree to which attaining one goal negates or subverts attaining another).

The second attribute of goals, intensity, pertains to the process of setting the goal or of determining how to reach it. Intensity would be measured by such factors as the scope of the cognitive process, the degree of effort required, the importance of the goal, and the context in which it is set. Goal intensity may be related to goal content; for example, a more intense psychological process is needed to set complex goals and to figure out how to attain them than the process needed to set and attain simple goals. Goal intensity has not been studied as such, although a related concept, goal commitment, has been measured in a number of experiments.

Relation of Goal Dimensions to Performance

Goal Difficulty

In an earlier review of the goal-setting literature, Locke (1968) found evidence for a positive, linear relation between goal difficulty and task performance (assuming sufficient ability), and more recent studies have supported these findings. Four results in three experimental field studies demonstrated that harder goals led to better performance than easy goals: Latham and Locke (1975) with logging crews; Yukl and Latham (1978) with typists; and a simulated field study by Bassett (1979). In a separate manipulation, Bassett also found that shorter time limits led to a faster work pace than longer time limits.

Twenty-five experimental laboratory studies have obtained similar results with a wide variety of tasks: Bavelas (1978), with a figure-selection task; Bavelas and Lee (1978) in five of six experiments involving brainstorming, figure selection, and sum estimation tasks; Campbell and Ilgen (1976) with chess; Hannan (1975) with a coding (credit applications) task; LaPorte and Nath (1976) with prose learning; Latham and Saari (1979b) with brainstorming; Locke and Bryan (1969b) with simple addition; Locke, Cartledge, and Knerr (1970) in four studies, three with reaction time and one with simple addition; Locke, Mento, and Katcer (1978) with perceptual speed; London and Oldham (1976) with card sorting; Masters, Furman, and Barden (1977) in two studies of four- and five-year-old children working on a color discrimination task; Mento, Cartledge, and Locke (1980) in two experiments using a perceptual speed task; Rothkopf and Billington (1975) and Rothkopf and Kaplan (1972) in more complex prose-learning studies than that of LaPorte and Nath (1976); and Sales (1970), using anagrams. In Sales's study, task rather than goal difficulty was manipulated by means of varying the work load given to the subjects. Presumably subjects developed implicit goals based on the amount of work assigned to them. Ness and Patton (1979) also found that a harder task led to beter weight-lifting performance than an easier task when subjects were deceived as to the actual weights.

Four studies found conditional[3] support for a positive relation between goal difficulty and performance. Becker (1978) with an energy conservation task, Erez (1977) with a clerical task, and Strang, Lawrence, and Fowler (1978) with a computation task, all found that only subjects who had high goals and who received feedback regarding their performance in relation to those goals performed better than subjects with low goals. This pattern of results seems also to have been present in Frost and Mahoney's (1976) first study using a reading task (see their Table 1, p. 339). Subjects with high and moderately high goals who apparently received frequent feedback performed better than those with average goals, whereas the opposite pattern was obtained for subjects given no feedback during the forty-two-minute work period (interaction $p = .11$; t tests were not performed).

Six experimental laboratory studies found no relation betwen goal level and task performance. Bavelas and Lee (1978) allowed only fifteen minutes for an addition task and gave subjects no information either before or during the task of how fast they needed to go to attain the goal. Frost and Mahoney (1976) found negative results with a jigsaw puzzle task, although their range of goal difficulty was limited: from medium to hard to very hard (actual probabilities of success were .50, .135, and .026, respectively). The same narrow range of difficulty (very difficult to moderately difficult) may explain the negative results of Oldham (1975) using a time sheet computation task. Moreover, not all subjects accepted the assigned goals in that study, and it is not clear that ability was controlled when Oldham (1975, pp. 471–472) did his post hoc analysis by personal goal level. Organ (1977) also compared moderate goals with hard goals using an anagram task. However, since no group average even reached the level of the moderate goal, the hard goal may have been totally unrealistic.

The fifth negative study, by Motowidlo, Loehr, and Dunnette (1978), using a complex computation task, examined the goal theory–expectancy theory controversy. Goal theory predicts that harder goals lead to better performance than easy goals, despite their lower probability of being fully reached. In contrast, expectancy theory predicts (other things being equal) a positive relation between expectancy and performance, the opposite of the goal theory prediction. Motowidlo et al. found a positive relation between expectancy and performance, which is in agreement with expectancy theory. One possible confounding factor is that the subjects in the Motowidlo et al. study did not make their expectancy ratings conditional upon trying their hardest to reach the goal or to win (pointed out by Mento et al., 1980, based on Yates and Kulick, 1977, among others). Thus, low expectancy ratings could mean that a subject was not planning to exert maximum effort, whereas high ratings would mean the opposite. This would yield a spurious positive correlation between expectancy and performance. Furthermore, Motowidlo et al. did not provide their subjects with feedback regarding how close they were coming to their goals during task performance. (The importance of this factor is documented below.) The two studies by Mento et al. (1980), which avoided the errors of the Motowidlo et al. study and incorporated other methodological improvements, found the usual positive relation between goal level and performance and no relation between expectancy and performance.

Forward and Zander (1971) used goals set by groups of high school boys on a team-coding task as both independent and dependent variables. Success and failure as well as outside pressures were covertly manipulated to influence goal setting, which occurred before each trial of the task. Under these somewhat complex conditions, goal discrepancy (goal minus previous performance level) was either unrelated or negatively related to subsequent performance.

The results of the experimental studies were, to varying degrees, supported by the results of fifteen correlational studies. Andrews and Farris (1972) found that time pressure was associated with high performance among scientists and engineers. Hall and Lawler (1971), with a similar sample, found no relation between time pressure and performance but found a significant relation between both quality and financial pressure (implied goals?) and work performance. Ashworth and Mobley[4] found a significant relation between performance goal level and training performance for Marine recruits. Blumenfeld and Leidy (1969), in what also could be called a natural field experiment, found that soft-drink servicemen who were assigned higher goals serviced more machines than those assigned lower goals. Hamner and Harnett (1974) found that subjects in an experimental study of bargaining who expected (tried?) to earn a high amount of money earned more than those who expected (tried?) to earn less money. Locke et al. (1970), in the last of their five studies, found a significant correlation between grade goals on an hourly exam and actual grade earned.

The majority of the correlational studies found only a conditional positive relation between goal difficulty and performance and/or effort. Carroll and Tosi (1970) found a positive relation only for managers who were mature and high in self-assurance; Dachler and Mobley (1973) found it only for production workers (in two plants) with long tenure (one or two years or more); Dossett, Latham, and Mitchell (1979), found it in two studies of clerical personnel, but only for those who set goals participatively; Hall and Hall (1976) found it for the class performance of second through fourth grade students in high-support schools; and Ivancevich and McMahon (1977a, 1977b, 1977c) found it for skilled technicians who had higher order (growth) need strength, were white, and had higher levels of education.

Negative results were obtained by Forward and Zander (1971) with United Fund campaign workers, Hall and Foster (1977) with participants in a simulated management game, and Steers (1975) with first-level supervisors.

All the correlational studies are, of course, open to multiple causal interpretations. For example, Dossett et al. (1979) implied that their results may be an artifact of ability, since ability was considered when setting goals in the participative groups but not in the assigned groups. In fact, none of the correlational studies had controls for ability. Also, many relied on self-ratings of goal difficulty or performance. The Yukl and Latham (1978) study found that only objective goal level, not subjective goal difficulty, was related to typing performance. None of the correlational studies measured the individual's personal goal level, a measure that Metno et al. (1980) found to be the single best motivational predictor of performance. Their measures of subjective goal difficulty did not explain any variance in performance over and above that explained by objective and personal goal levels.

Goal Specificity

Specific Hard Goals Versus "Do Best" Goals or No Goals. Previous research found that specific, challenging (difficult) goals led to higher output than vague goals such as "do your best" (Locke, 1968). Subsequent research has strongly supported these results, although in a number of studies, no distinction was made between groups told to do their best and those assigned no specific goals. The latter were typically labeled *no goal* groups. We have not found any differences in the results obtained by studies in which no goals are assigned and those in which subjects are explicitly told to do their best. No goal subjects, it appears, typically try to do as well as they can on the assigned task.

Twenty-four field experiments all found that individuals given specific, challenging goals either outperformed those trying to do their best or surpassed their own previous performance when they were not trying for specific goals: Bandura and Simon (1977) with dieting; Dockstader[5] with key punching; Dossett et al.(1979) in two studies, one using a clerical test and the other performance evaluations for clerical workers; Ivancevich (1977) with maintenance technicians; Ivancevich (1974) in two plants with marketing and production workers (for one or more performance criteria); Ivancevich (1976) with sales personnel; Kim and Hamner (1976) with telephone service jobs; Kolb and Boyatzis (1970) with personality change in a T-group; Latham and Baldes (1975) with truck loading; Latham and Kinne (1974) with logging; and Latham and Yukl (1975a) with wood workers who participated in goal setting; Latham and Yukl (1976) with typing; Latham, Mitchell, and Dossett (1978) with engineering and scientific work; Migliore (1977) with canning (press department) and ship loading (two studies); Nemeroff and Cosentino (1979) with performance appraisal activities; Umstot, Bell, and Mitchell (1976) with coding land parcels; Wexley and Nemeroff (1975) with managerial training; and White, Mitchell, and Bell (1977) with card sorting. The studies by Adam (1975) with die casters, Feeney with customer service workers ("At Emery Air Freight," 1973), and Komaki, Barwick, and Scott (1978) with pastry workers are also included in this group. Although these investigations claimed that they were doing behavior modification, the major technique actually used was goal setting plus feedback regarding goal attainment (Locke, 1977).

A negative result was obtained by Latham and Yukl (1975a) with one sample of woods workers. Either individual differences or lack of organizational support may have been responsible for this failure.

(Ivancevich, 1974, also cited differences in organizational support as the reason for obtaining better results in one of his plants than the other.)

The generally positive results of the field studies were supported by the results of twenty laboratory studies: Chung and Vickery (1976; their KR condition included implicit goal setting) with a clerical task; Frost and Mahoney (1976) with a reading task (but only for subjects given frequent feedback) and with a puzzle task; Hannan (1975) with a coding task; Kaplan and Rothkopf (1974) and LaPorte and Nath (1976) with prose learning; Latham and Saari (1979a) with brainstorming; Latham and Saari (1979b) with brainstorming again, but only for subjects who set goals participatively (though this may have been an artifact since the authors reported that the assigned goal subjects may not have understood the instructions clearly); Locke and Bryan (1969a) with a driving task; Locke et al. (1978) with perceptual speed (comparing the hard-goal vs. do-best groups only); Mossholder (1980) using two assembly tasks; Organ (1977) with anagrams; Pritchard and Curtis (1973) with card sorting; Reynolds, Standiford, and Anderson (1979) with learning prose; Rosswork (1977) with a sentence construction task used with sixth graders; Rothkopf and Billington (1975) and Rothkopf and Kaplan (1972), again with learning prose; Strang, Lawrence, and Fowler (1978) with arithmetic computation (but only for hard-goal subjects who had feedback); and Terborg and Miller (1978) with tinkertoy assembly.

A negative result was obtained by Organ (1977) on a proofreading task. Evidently the goals set were moderate rather than hard, since they were set at the median scores for pretest subjects and were surpassed by subjects in all conditions. Moderate goals are not predicted to lead to higher performance than do-best goals. Locke et al. (1978), for example, found that although hard-goal subjects exceeded the performance of do-best subjects, moderate-goal subjects did not.

Seven correlational field studies also supported or partially supported the superiority of specific hard goals over do-best goals or no goals; Blumenfeld and Leidy (1969) with soft drink servicemen; Brass and Oldham (1976) and Oldham (1976) with foremen; Burke and Wilcox (1969) with telephone operators; Ronan, Latham, and Kinne (1973) with pulpwood producers; Steers (1975) with supervisors (but only those high on need for achievement); and Terborg (1976) with students studying programmed texts.

Clear versus unclear goals or intentions. Relatively few studies have been concerned with the effect of goal clarity on performance. Two experimental studies (Kaplan and Rothkopf, 1974; Rothkopf and Kaplan, 1972) found that specific prose-learning goals led to more learning than generally stated goals. Carroll and Tosi (1970) found that goal clarity correlated with increased effort only for managers who were mature and decisive and who had low job interest and low support from their managers. Ivancevich and McMahon (1977a, 1977b, 1977c) found that goal clarity correlated with performance mainly for technicians who were black, less educated, and high on higher order need strength. These correlational studies seem to provide no consistent pattern, which is not surprising in view of the problems inherent in concurrent, self-report designs.

The borderline and negative results of Hall and Hall (1976) and Hall and Foster (1977) with respect to goal difficulty and performance may have been because their goals did not consist of clear objectives but of the self-rated strength of the subjects' intentions to perform well.

The findings of these studies involving vague intentions can be contrasted with the organizational studies by H. Miller, Katerberg, and Hulin (1979), Mobley, Horner, and Hollingsworth (1978), and Mobley, Hand, Baker, and Meglino (1979). They found significant longitudinal correlations between the specific intention to remain in or leave the organization and the corresponding action.

Conclusions

Overall, forty-eight studies partly or wholly supported the hypothesis that hard goals lead to better performance than medium or easy goals; nine studies failed to support it. Fifty-one studies partially or wholly supported the view that specific hard goals lead to better performance than do-your-best or no goals; two studies did not support it. Combining these two sets of studies, we found that ninety-nine out of 110 studies found that specific, hard goals produced better performance than medium, easy, do-your-best, or no goals. This represents a success rate of 90 percent.

Most of these studies (at least the experimental ones) were well designed; they included control groups, random assignment, negligible attrition, controls for ability, objective performance measures, and a great variety of tasks and situation. Thus, considerable confidence can be placed in them in terms of both internal and external validity.

Mechanisms for Goal-Setting Effects

Given that goal setting works, it is relevant to ask how it affects task performance. We view goal setting primarily as a motivational mechanism (although cognitive elements are necessarily involved). The concept of motivation is used to explain the direction, amplitude (effort), and duration (persistence) of action. Not surprisingly, all three are affected by goal setting. One additional, indirect mechanism is also described.

Direction

Most fundamentally, goals direct attention and action. Perhaps the most obvious demonstration of this mechanism is the study by Locke and Bryan (1969a) in which drivers were given feedback regarding five different dimensions of driving performance but were assigned goals with respect to only one dimension. The dimension for which a goal was assigned showed significantly more improvement that the remaining dimensions. Similarly, Locke et al. (1970) found that subjects modified their speed of reaction (to make it faster or slower) on a simple reaction-time task in the direction of their overall objective. Reynolds et al. (1979) found that subjects spent more time reading prose passages that were relevant to their goals (consisting of questions inserted in the text) than to reading parts that were not relevant. Terborg (1976) found that subjects with specific goals spent a greater percentage of the time looking at the text material to be learned than did subjects with nonspecific goals or no goals. (Terborg labeled this measure *effort* in his study.) Rothkopf and Billington (1979) found that subjects with specific learning goals, as compared with subjects with no specific learning goals (do-your-best instructions), spent an equal or greater amount of time inspecting passages with goal-relevant material and significantly less time looking at incidental passages.

Effort

Since different goals may require different amounts of effort, effort is mobilized simultaneously with direction in proportion to the perceived requirements of the goal or task. Thus, as Kahneman (1973) and Shapira[2] have argued, more effort is expended on hard tasks (which are accepted) than on easy tasks. Sales (1970) found that higher work loads produce higher subjective effort, faster heart rates, and higher output per unit time than lower work loads. Latham and Locke (1975) and Bassett (1979) found that people work faster under shorter than under longer time limits. In summary, higher goals produce higher performance than lower goals or no goals because people simply work harder for the former (Locke, 1968; Terborg, 1976; Terborg and Miller, 1978; for earlier documentation see Locke and Bryan, 1966).

This hypothesis of a positive linear relation between motivation or effort and performance (also stated in Locke, 1968, and Yates and Kulick 1977), contradicts the Yerkes–Dodson inverted-U "law," which asserts that performance is maximal at moderate levels of motivation. Although it is true that with any given subject, performance eventually will level off as the limit of capacity or ability is reached (Bavelas and Lee, 1978; Kahneman, 1973), this is a separate issue from that of motivation. Of course, subjects may abandon their goals if they become too difficult, but the hypothesized function assumes goal commitment. Performance may also drop if subjects become highly anxious, especially on a complex or underlearned task. But a state of high anxiety should not be labeled *high motivation* in the positive sense because it represents a state of conflict rather than of single-minded goal pursuit.

Persistence

Persistence is nothing more than directed effort extended over time; thus, it is a combination of the previous two mechanisms. Most laboratory experiments on goal setting have not been designed to allow for the measurement of persistence effects, since time limits typically have been imposed; field studies to date have measured only the end results of goal setting rather than how they were obtained. LaPorte and Nath (1976) allowed some subjects unlimited time to red a prose passsage. Those asked to read the passage to get 90 percent of twenty postreading questions correct spent more time on the passage than subjects asked to get 25 percent of the postreading questions correct. Rothkopf and Billington (1979) found that more time was spent on goal-relevant than on incidental passages. More studies of this type would be highly desirable.

Strategy Development

Whereas the first three mechanisms are relatively direct in their effects, this last mechanism is indirect. It involves developing strategies or action plans for attaining one's goals. Although strategy development is motivated by goals, the mechanism itself is cognitive in essence; it involves skill development or creative problem solving.

Bandura and Simon (1977), for example, found that dieting subjects with specific quotas for number of mouthfuls eaten changed their eating patterns (for instance, by eating more low-calorie foods that did not count in their quotas). They also engaged in more planning (for instance, by saving part of their quota for a dinner out). Latham and Baldes (1975) observed that some of the truck drivers assigned specific hard goals with respect to truck weight recommended minor modifications of their trucks to help them increase the accuracy of their judgments of weight.

In Terborg's (1976) study, the subjects who set specific goals were more likely to employ relevant learning strategies (for instance, writing notes in the margins) than those who did not set goals. A unique aspect of Terborg's (1976) design was that he was able to obtain separate measures of direction of effort (which he called "effort") and of strategy use (which he called "direction"). He found that when these mechanisms were partialed out, there was no relation between goals and task performance. This supports the argument that these are some of the mechanisms by which goals affect performance.

In a similar vein, Kolb and Boyatzis (1970) found that behavior change in a T-group was greatest for participants who developed plans for evaluating their performance in relation to their goals. Such plans evidently were developed only for behavior dimensions that the subjects were trying to change.

Bavelas and Lee (1978) made detailed analyses in three experiments to determine the strategies subjects used to attain hard goals. They found that subjects would frequently redefine the task in a way that would permit them to give "looser" or lower quality answers. For example, subjects asked to list very large numbers of "white, hard, edible objects" were more likely to list objects that were white but not very hard or hard but not very edible than were subjects given easier goals. Similarly, with appropriate training, subjects given hard addition goals would more often estimate rather than calculate their answers as compared to subjects with easy goals.

Subjects given hard goals in Rosswork's (1977) study simply wrote shorter sentences to meet their quota, which was expressed in terms of total sentences written. The subjects in Sales's (1970) study who were given a high work load made more errors, presumably by lowering their standards, than those given a low work load. Christensen-Szalanski (1980) found that subjects who were given a short time limit in problem solving used less complex and less adequate strategies than subjects given a longer time limit. Strategy development is especially important in complex tasks. If the requisite strategies are not developed, the increased motivation provided by the goals will not be translated into effective performance.

We now examine the influence of feedback, money, and participation on the effectiveness of goal setting.

Knowledge of Results (Feedback)

In early goal-setting studies, attempts were made to separate the effects of feedback (that is, knowledge of results [KR]) from the effects of goal setting to determine whether KR directly influenced performance or whether its effects were mediated by goal-setting activity (Locke, 1967; Locke & Bryan, 1968, 1969a, 1969b; Locke, Cartledge, & Koeppel, 1968). In the most carefully controlled of these studies, all subjects with specific goals also received knowledge of their performance in relation to their goals; individuals in the KR conditions received knowledge of their actual scores presented in such a way as to preclude their use in setting goals. Such knowledge of scores did not lead to better performance than no knowledge of scores. The evidence from these and related studies indicated that knowledge of scores was not sufficient to improve task performance. However, since groups with goals and no KR were not included, these studies did not test the possibility that KR may be a necessary condition for goals to affect performance. Few studies relevant to this hypothesis had been conducted at the time of the Latham and Yukl (1975b) review.

A number of such studies have since been completed in both the laboratory and the field. Figure 2–1 illustrates the conditions of interest. Cell 1 represents specific, hard goals combined with KR; cell 2, specific, hard goals with out KR; cell 3, KR with no specific goals (or do-best goals that are equivalent to no assigned goals); and cell 4, neither specific goals nor KR.

	KR	No KR
Specific hard goal	1	2
No specific goal or do-best goal	3	4

Figure 2–1. Model for Analyzing goal–KR studies. (KR = knowledge of results.)

The studies reviewed here included at least three of the four cells in figure 2–1. Table 2–1 summarizes the results of these comparisons.

Two types of studies are evident in table 2–1. The first set consists of comparisons between cells 1, 3, and 4. Consistent with Locke's (1968) mediating hypothesis, these studies indicate that although KR alone is not sufficient to improve performance (3 = 4), KR plus goals results in performance increases (1 > 3).

In a study of overweight clients in a weight clinic, participants who kept daily records of all the food they consumed but did not set goals to reduce food intake did not alter their eating habits and performed no differently from a control group who kept no records and set no specific goals (Bandura & Simon, 1977). However, participants who set goals based on their daily records significantly decreased food consumption compared with the KR-only group.

Dockstader[5] found no apparent effect of KR alone on the performance of key punch operators, but those provided with KR and a performance standard significantly exceeded their own previous performance and that of the KR-only group.

Latham et al. (1978) found no differences between engineers and scientists with do-best goals who were provided with feedback concerning their performance on certain appraisal criteria and those who received no feedback; however, the subjects who set or were assigned specific, hard goals in response to the feedback performed significantly better than those in the do-best and control groups.

Table 2–1
Studies Comparing the Effects of Goals and KR on Performance

	Comparison Performed			
Study	*1 vs. 2*	*1 vs. 3*	*2 vs. 4*	*3 vs. 4*
Bandura & Simon (1977)		1 > 3		3 = 4
Dockstader		1 > 3		3 = 4
Latham, Mitchell, & Dossett (1978)		1 > 3		3 = 4
Nemeroff & Cosentino (1979)		1 > 3		3 = 4
"At Emery Air Freight" (1973)	1 > 2		2 = 4	
Komaki, Barwick, & Scott (1978)	1 > 2		2 = 4	
Becker (1978)[a]	1 > 2		2 = 4	
Strang, Lawrence, & Fowler (1978)[a]	1 > 2		2 > 4[b]	

Note: KR = knowledge of results. 1 = specific, hard goals combined with KR; 2 = specific, hard goals without KR; 3 = KR with no specific goals (or do-best goals); 4 = neither specific goals nor KR.

[a]Included both hard and easy goal plus KR conditions. The performance of easy-goal subjects was no better than that in the control condition.

[b]Results differed, depending on performance criterion utilized.

Nemeroff and Cosentino (1979) found that supervisors who were provided with feedback concerning their behavior during performance appraisal sessions but who did not use the KR to set specific goals did not improve subsequent performance. Those supervisors who set specific goals in response to the feedback performed significantly better on the twelve behaviors for which they set goals and conducted significantly more successful appraisal interviews.

This first set of studies demonstrates that KR without goals is not sufficient to improve performance (3 = 4), but given KR, goals are sufficient for performance to be improved (1 > 3). Thus, goals seem necessary for KR to improve performance.

The second set of studies consists of comparisons between cells 1, 2, and 4. In what was called a "positive reinforcement" program ("At Emery Air Freight," 1973), employees in the customer service department and on the shipping docks were given a group-performance goal, progress toward the goal was posted, and each employee also kept a personal record of performance. Performance levels increased markedly, but when KR was removed and self-reports were not kept, employee performance returned to baseline levels "or was almost as bad" ("At Emery Air Freight," 1973, p. 45), even though the performance target remained in effect (1 > 2, 2 = 4).

In another behavior modification program (actually a goals and KR study; see Locke, 1980), Komaki, Barwick, and Scott (1978) examined safe behavior in the making and wrapping of pastry products. The authors introduced a specific, hard safety goal and displayed performance results on a graph in view of all the workers. Substantial performance improvements occurred, but when the KR was eliminated in a reversal phase, performance returned to baseline levels.

In a study of residential electricity use, Becker (1978) manipulated specific goals and KR. Families included in his study represent cells 1, 2, and 4 of figure 2–1; he also included easy-goal groups with and without KR. The only families whose conservation performance improved significantly from baseline levels were those with hard goals plus KR. All other groups performed no better than a control group. Strang et al. (1978) conducted a laboratory study utilizing a design similar to Becker's (cells 1, 2, and 4 plus the same two easy-goal conditions as above). Subjects worked on an arithmetic computation task. The performance of subjects with hard goals and feedback was significantly better than that of the goals-only subjects (1 > 2). Using time to finish as a criterion, there were no differences between the performance of the goals-only subjects and that of control group subjects (2 = 4). In terms of number of errors, however, the control group's performance was significantly better than that of the goals-only group

(4 > 2), suggesting that goals without KR may even inhibit accurate performance.

The results of this second group of studies indicate that goals without KR are not sufficient to improve performance (2 = 4), but given goals, KR is sufficient to effect performance improvement (1 > 2). Thus, KR seems necessary for goals to affect performance.

Although her study is not included in table 2–1 because she used a correlational analysis, Erez (1977) was the first to suggest that KR is a necessary condition for the goal-performance relation. In her laboratory study, subjects worked on a number comparison task. At the end of one performance trial, they set goals for a second trial. Half of the subjects were provided with KR at the end of the first trial and half were not. Erez used a multiple regression analysis to identify the unique contribution of the Goal × KR interaction. The regression equation included Stage 1 performance, the two main effects variables (goals, KR), and the Goal × KR interaction. When all four variables were placed in the regression simultaneously, the interaction effect was significant, but beta weights for goals and KR were not significantly different from zero. The goal–performance correlation in the KR group was .60 and in the no-KR group, .01. These findings led Erez to conclude that KR is necessary for goals to affect performance.

Kim and Hamner's (1976) study of goals and feedback was not included in this analysis because they acknowledged that their goals-only group actually may have received informal feedback. Thus, their study only includes two cells: cell 1, with different groups having different amounts and types of feedback, and cell 4, which comprised the "before" scores of the various groups. In this study, as in the one by Frost and Mahoney (1976, Task A), providing explicit or frequent feedback clearly facilitated performance.

Integrating the two sets of studies points to one unequivocal conclusion: neither KR alone nor goals alone is sufficient to improve performance. Both are necessary. This view of goals and feedback as reciprocally dependent seems more useful and more accurate than Locke's (1968) earlier position, which viewed goals as mediating the effects of feedback on performance. Together, goals and feedback appear sufficient to improve task performance (given the obvious contextual variables such as adequate ability and lack of external blocks to performance). The studies demonstrate that action is regulated by both cognition (knowledge) and motivation.

Table 2–1 demonstrates that not a single study was designed to allow all of the four possible comparisons. In other words, no study involved a complete 2 × 2 design with KR/no-KR and specific, hard goals/"do-best" goals, or no goals as the variables. Even the studies reported did not always involve total control over the variables; for example, spontaneous goal setting among KR-only subjects was not always prevented. Such a complete, controlled study is now being conducted by two of the present authors. It is predicted that cell 1 (see figure 2-1) will show better performance than the remaining cells, which should not differ among themselves. This would parallel the results of Becker (1978) and Strang et al. (1978) using KR/no-KR and hard/easy goal conditions.

Other issues remain to be explored regarding the role of KR. For example, Cummings, Schwab, and Rosen (1971) found that providing KR can lead to the setting of higher goals than not providing KR; this indicates that subjects may underestimate their capacity without correct information about their previous performance. Related to this, Greller (1980) found that supervisors incorrectly estimated the importance of various sources of feedback to subordinates. These issues deserve further study.

One issue that does not seem to deserve further study is that of feedback as a reinforcer. The findings and arguments of Annett (1969), Bandura (1977), and Locke (1977, 1980) speak convincingly against the thesis that feedback conditions behavior. It seems more useful and valid to treat feedback or KR as information, the effect of which depends on how it is processed (see Locke, Cartledge, and Koeppel, 1968).

A recent article (Ilgen, Fisher, and Taylor, 1979) specifies several dimensions along which KR can vary: amount, type, frequency, specificity, timing, source, sign, and recency. Experimental studies of these dimensions could reveal the most effective form in which to provide KR in conjunction with goals. Unfortunately, the studies to date have not been systematic enough to allow any conclusions about these dimensions.

Our major conclusion, that both goals and KR are necessary to improve performance, provides a clear prescription for task management. Not only should specific, hard goals be established, but KR should be provided to show performance in relation to these goals. The "At Emery Air Freight" (1973), Komaki et al. (1978), Latham and Kinne (1974), and Latham and Baldes (1975) studies emphasize how inexpensive such goals-plus-KR programs can be in field settings relative to their benefits.

Monetary Rewards

It is known that money can be a powerful motivator of performance. Locke, Feren, McCaleb, Shaw, and Denny (1980), for example, found that individual money incentives increased worker performance by a median of 30 percent. Locke (1968) argued that goal setting may be one mechanism by which money affects task performance.

There are several possible ways that this might occur. First, money could affect the level at which goals are set or the level at which intentions are established. In five studies, Locke, Bryan, and Kendall (1968) found that in some cases, money did affect goal or intention level. Furthermore, in line with the mediating hypothesis, goals and intentions affected performance even when the effects of incentives were partialed out, whereas incentives were unrelated to performance when goal and intention level were controlled.

Generally these results have not been replicated. For example, Pritchard and Curtis (1973) found that although there was no difference in the performance effects of no incentive versus a small incentive, subjects who were offered high incentives performed better on a sorting task than those offered small or no incentives even when goal level was controlled. Similarly, Terborg (1976) found that partialing out the effects of self-set goals in a programmed learning task failed to vitiate the difference between contingent and noncontingent pay on performance. Terborg and Miller (1978) found similar results using a toy assembly task, assigned goals, and piece-rate versus hourly pay. Latham et al. (1978) found a significant main effect for an anticipated monetary bonus independent of a significant goal-level effect on the job performance of engineers and scientists. In all four of these studies, goals and money had independent effects on performance. This was also the case in London and Oldham's (1976) study, although their incentive effects were not easily interpretable. Chung and Vickery (1976) also found independent effects for money and goals (their KR condition included a goal-setting treatment).

A second possibility is that money might induce more spontaneous goal setting than would occur without incentives. In support of this hypothesis, Saari and Latham[6] found that the introduction of an incentive system led mountain beaver trappers to set specific goals for themselves. However, in the laboratory studies by Terborg (1976) and Terborg and Miller (1978), incentive pay did not lead to more specific goal setting than hourly pay.

A third possibility, which was stressed by Locke (1968), is that rather than increasing the likelihood of spontaneous goal setting or increasing the level at which goals are set (a hypothesis that has not yet been fully tested), incentives affect the individual's degree of goal commitment. In other words, offering money may arouse the willingness to expend more effort to attain a given objective than not offering money. In terms of expectancy theory, money rewards endow goal success with a higher valence or value than no money. This is our interpretation of the results obtained by Latham et al. (1978), London and Oldham (1976), Pritchard and Curtis (1973), Terborg (1976), and Terborg and Miller (1978).

Attempts to measure this commitment effect through self reports have not been successful (for example, Latham et al., 1978; Pritchard and Curtis, 1973). The whole issue of why goal commitment measures have not been related to performance in goal-setting research will be discussed at length in a later section of this article.

The effectiveness of money in mobilizing effort undoubtedly depends on the amount of money offered. Pritchard and Curtis (1973) found an incentive effect only when they offered $3 compared with 50¢ or no money at all for ten minutes of work. Similarly, Rosswork (1977) found a substantial goal effect but no incentive effect when school children were offered up to 6¢ for each sentence composed during two five-minute periods.

The findings indicate that money can affect task performance independently of goal level. The most plausible mechanism for this effect appears to be goal commitment, with the degree of increased commitment depending on the amount of the incentive offered. Although direct questions regarding commitment used in several studies do not support this interpretation, the fault may lie in poor experimental design, poor measures, or poor introspection by subjects (issues we discuss later). Incentives may also increase the likelihood of spontaneous goal setting or of setting high goals, but there has not yet been enough research to provide support for these mechanisms.

Participation and Supportiveness

Participation has long been recommended by social scientists as a means of obtaining employee commitment to organizational goals and of reducing resistance to change. Nevertheless, an extensive review of the participation in decision-making literature by Locke and Schweiger (1979) found no consistent difference in the effectiveness of top-down ("autocratic") decision making and decisions made with subordinate participation. We specifically review those studies that involved participation in goal setting.

Carroll and Tosi (1970) included a measure of perceived participation in goal setting in a questionnaire administered at a manufacturing firm that had a Management by Objectives program. The results indicated that participation did not correlate significantly with employee perceptions of goal attainment or employee perception of increases in effort.

Negative results were also obtained in a field experiment by Ivancevich (1976). This study compared participative and assigned goal setting for sales personnel. Goals were set for each of four quantitative performance criteria. Although both goal-setting groups showed performance increases, no significant differences in performance were found between the participative and assigned goal conditions.

In a second study, Ivancevich (1977) obtained mixed results with maintenance department technicians. Four performance variables were measured. With regard to service complaints and costs, the assigned goal-setting group showed more improvement than the participative group; however, for safety the participative goal group performed better than the assigned group. There was no significant difference between the two groups in absenteeism.

A possible drawback of these studies is that goal difficulty levels were not assessed for the different goal groups. Conceivably, goal difficulty could have been confounded with the assigned versus participative manipulations.

The following studies all included measurements of goal difficulty. In a field experiment involving logging crews, Latham and Yukl (1975a) found that participative goal setting resulted in higher performance than assigned goal setting for uneducated (less than nine years of education) loggers in the South. The superiority of participative goal setting may have been due in part to the higher goals that were set in the participative rather than the assigned condition.

In a second field experiment, Latham and Yukl (1976) found no significant differences in the performance of typists with participative and assigned goals. Consistent with these results, there was no difference in the difficulty levels of the goals in each condition. Both groups, however, improved their performance significantly after specific goals had been set.

Latham et al. (1978) found that engineers and scientists in a participative goal condition set more difficult goals than their peers who had assigned goals. However, the perceptions of goal difficulty did not differ, and no significant differences in goal acceptance were found between the two goal conditions. The participative and assigned groups did not differ significantly in performance, although only the participative group significantly outperformed the control group.

These three studies indicate that participation in goal setting may affect performance through its influence on goal difficulty. Thus, if goal difficulty is held constant, participation should not affect performance. Participation may affect performance only if it leads to higher goals being set than is the case when a supervisor assigns them unilaterally.

Latham and Saari (1979a) systematically tested this hypothesis in a laboratory study using a brainstorming task. Goal difficulty levels were held constant across the participative and assigned goal conditions. As predicted, no significant differences in performance were found between the two goal setting groups. Moreover, no difference on a measure of goal acceptance was found.

Dossett et al. (1979) replicated this finding in two field experiments involving testing and performance appraisal. In the first experiment employees who participated in setting their goals on a test attained the same performance level as individuals who were assigned goals of the same difficulty level. This same finding was obtained in a second study, which involved setting goals on a performance appraisal form.

Hannan (1975), using a simulated credit application evaluation task, also found that assigned and participatively set goals led to the same level of performance when goal level was controlled. (There was a small Goal × Participation interaction, however.)

Likert[7] has pointed out that when assigned goal setting is effective, it may be because the supervisors who assign the goals behave in a supportive manner. Latham and Saari (1979b) tested this assumption in a second laboratory study using a brainstorming task. Goal difficulty again was held constant between the participative and assigned goal groups. However, the supportiveness of the experimenter was varied. The results indicated that a supportive supervisory style led to higher goals being set than a nonsupportive style. It was also found that it took significantly longer to set goals in the participative goal conditions than in the assigned conditions because the subjects asked more questions regarding what answers were acceptable. Latham and Saari (1979b) concluded that the importance of participation in goal setting may be that it not only leads to the setting of high goals but it can also lead to increased understanding of how to attain them—two variables that can have a direct impact on performance.

Although few consistent differences in task performance appear between assigned and participatively set goal groups, several tentative conclusions regarding the influence of participation can be drawn. There appear to be two possible mechanisms by which participation could affect task motivation. First, it can lead to the setting of higher goals than would be the case without participation, although theoretically, assigned goals can be set at any level the supervisor or experimenter chooses. Second, participation could, in some cases, lead to greater goal acceptance or commitment than assigned goals. The first effect has been found twice (Latham et al., 1978; Latham and Yukl, 1975a). (We discuss the second effect in the section on goal acceptance.)

It may be that supportiveness, as discussed in studies by Latham and Saari (1979b), Hall and Hall (1976), and Ivancevich (1974, who called it "reinforcement"), is more crucial than participation in achieving goal acceptance. Participation itself, of course, may entail supportiveness. Other factors, such as the power of the supervisors and the rewards and punishments given for goal attainment and nonattainment, also may be important, but these have not been systematically investigated.

Further, it is possible that the motivational effects of participation are not as important in gaining performance improvement as are its cognitive effects. Locke et al. (1980) found that the single most successful field experiment on participation to date stressed the cognitive benefits; participation was used to get good ideas from workers as to how to improve performance efficiency (Bragg and Andrews, 1973). The potential cognitive benefits of participation are discussed in some detail in Locke and Schweiger (1979) and were implied in the Latham and Saari (1979b) study.

Individual Differences

Thus far we have been discussing goal setting as though it affected every individual in the same manner. To date, individual differences have received minimal attention in the goal-setting literature, although several variables have been examined in one or more studies.

Demographic Variables

Of the few goal-setting studies that have investigated demographic variables, most have dealt with the effects of education, race, and job tenure.

Education. In a study involving electronics technicians, Ivancevich and McMahon (1977b) found that perceived goal challenge was significantly related to performance only for educated technicians (twelve years or more of education). In contrast, perceived goal clarity and goal feedback were significantly related to performance only for less educated technicians (fewer than twelve years of education).

In their field experiment with loggers, Latham and Yukl (1975a) compared assigned, participative, and do-best goal-setting conditions for educated white (12–16 years of education) and uneducated black (0–9 years of education) logging crews. Participative goal setting significantly affected the performance of the uneducated crews but did not affect the performance of the educated crews. The goal-setting program may not have been administered effectively in the latter sample, however; in addition, education was confounded with race.

These findings were not replicated in Latham and Yukl's (1976) field experiment involving female typists. In that study education did not moderate the effects of either participative or assigned goal setting. Similarly, Steers (1975) found no moderating effect of education on goal setting in a study of 113 female supervisors.

Although Latham et al. (1978) did not examine education as a moderator variable, we mention the study here because of the education level of the subjects: Goal setting had a significant effect on the performance of engineers and scientists with master's and doctoral degrees.

We must conclude that there is no consistent evidence for the effect of education as a moderator of goal setting, nor is there any convincing theoretical reason why there should be. Goal setting appears to be effective for individuals of all educational levels, ranging from elementary school children (Masters et al., 1977) to loggers with a mean education of 7.2 years (Latham and Yukl, 1975a) to engineers and scientists (Latham et al., 1978) with advanced degrees.

Race. As already noted, Latham and Yukl (1975a) found that less educated black loggers who participated in setting their goals were more productive and attained their goals more frequently than crews who were assigned goals by their supervisors or told to do their best. However, for the more educated white loggers there were no significant differences among the goal-setting conditions.

A study by Ivancevich and McMahon (1977a) of technicians supported these findings. Perceived participation in goal setting was related to several measures of performance for black technicians but not for whites. Goal clarity and feedback were also related to performance for blacks only, whereas goal challenge was related to performance for the whites only. Perhaps goal clarity, feedback, and participation affected the performance of blacks because, as Ivancevich and McMahon (1977a) stated,

it has been found that blacks have a higher need for security in performing their jobs. . . . One way to derive more security in a goal setting program is to have goal clarity, receive feedback, and participate in the process (p. 298).

Clearly, more studies are needed before this interpretation can be verified. If it is valid, then the racial factor would be reducible to a personality attribute that presumably would cut across racial lines.

Job Tenure. Five studies have examined tenure as a moderator variable in the goal-setting process. Three of them (Ivancevich and McMahon, 1977a; Latham and Yukl, 1976; Steers, 1975) found no moderating effect. Two studies by Dachler and Mobley (1973), found no significant relation between stated goals and productivity for short-tenure employees (less than 1–2 years), but a significant relation between these measures for long-tenure employees (1–2 or more years). Their explanation for this difference was that longer tenure employees have more accurate perceptions of their chances of reaching various levels of performance and of performance-outcome contingencies. Nevertheless, it is not clear why it would take one or more years for these perceptions to become accurate. In sum, the evidence to date does not show much promise with respect to job tenure as a moderator.

Age. In the study by Ivancevich and McMahon (1977b) on technicians, age was not related to goal setting or performance. To our knowledge no other studies have investigated the moderating effects of age. However, as previously noted, goal setting has been shown to be effective for children (for instance, Masters et al., 1977; Rosswork, 1977) as well as adults.

Sex. No study has systematically examined sex differences as a moderator of goal setting, though goal setting has been shown to significantly increase the performance of both males (e.g., Ivancevich and McMahon, 1977b; Latham and Yukl, 1975a) and females (Latham and Yukl, 1976; Steers, 1975).

Personality Variables

Need for Achievement. Steers (1975), in his study of female supervisors, found that performance was related to feedback and goal specificity only for high-need-achievement individuals. Participation in goal setting, on the other hand, was related to performance only among low-need-achievement supervisors. These findings indicate that high need achievers perform best when they are assigned specific goals and receive feedback on their progress toward these goals. Conversely, low need achievers (who are perhaps less confident) perform best when they are allowed to participate in the setting of their goals.

In his study using anagrams, Sales (1970) varied the work load given to subjects. Overall, productivity for subjects high in need for achievement was not higher than that for subjects low in need for achievement. However, an interaction occurred between work load and need for achievement. Sales reported a positive linear relation between need for achievement and productivity in the underload condition and a curvilinear (inverted-U) relation between need for achievement and productivity in the overload condition. Since high need achievers prefer goals of moderate difficulty, they presumably considered the overload condition too challenging for their liking.

In a laboratory experiment, Singh (1972) found that students with high need for achievement set higher goals for themselves over repeated trials of a mathematical clerical task than did low need achievers. Yukl and Latham (1978) obtained comparable results in their study involving typists. High need achievers who were allowed to participate in the goal-setting process set more difficult goals than did low-need-achievement typists, though they did not perform any better than low need achievers.

In the two experiments involving word processing operators, Dossett et al. (1979) found no moderating effects of need for achievement on performance appraisal measures or on performance on a selection test measuring mathematical ability. Goal difficulty was not examined in these studies because it was held constant across goal-setting conditions. Overall, the results again are inconsistent and unreliable.

Need for Independence. An earlier study by French, Kay, and Meyer (1966) found that employees with a high need for independence had greater goal acceptance when participation in goal setting was increased than when participation was reduced or not changed. Goal acceptance was not affected by changes in participation for employees with a low need for independence.

The moderating effect of need for independence has not been found by other researchers. For example, Searfoss and Monczka (1973) found no moderating effect of need for independence on the relationship between perceived participation on the part of managers in setting specific budgetary goals and subsequent motivation to achieve those goals. Similarly, in their study with typists, Latham and Yukl (1976) found that need for independence did not moderate the effects of either participative or assigned goal setting on performance. Dossett et al. (1979) also found no moderating effects of need for independence on the performance of word processing operators.

Higher Order Need Strength. Higher order need strength is defined as the degree to which a person desired enriched work (variety, autonomy, task identity, and feedback; see Hackman and Lawler, 1971). To our knowledge, only one study has examined this need as a possible moderator of goal setting.

In the study by Ivancevich and McMahon (1977c) involving technicians, initial analyses revealed no consistent relationships between various goal attributes and performance measures. However, when higher order need strength was used as a moderator, goal clarity, feedback, and challenge were related to effort (toward quantity and quality) and attendance for technicians with high higher order need strength. Conversely, for technicians with low higher order need strength, goal acceptance was related to effort (toward quality) and attendance. No obvious interpretation can be made of this finding.

Self-Esteem. In the study involving typists (Latham and Yukl, 1976), self-esteem did not moderate the effects of participative and assigned goal setting on performance. However, it was found that self-esteem and goal instrumentality interacted in their effects on performance (Yukl and Latham, 1978). Instrumentality was defined as "the extent to which desirable outcomes (for example, job security, pay, promotion) are perceived to be contingent upon goal attainment" (Yukl and Latham, 1978, p. 312). Specifically, when goal instrumentality was low (goal attainment not perceived as linked to important outcomes), typists with high self-esteem showed greater performance improvements than individuals with low self-esteem. There was no self-esteem effect when instrumentality was high. When self-esteem was low, typists who perceived high goal instrumentality showed greater performance improvement than those with low goal instrumentality; when self-esteem was high, there was no instrumentality effect. The integrating principle here may be that people with high self-esteem will work hard without practical rewards (for pride?), whereas people with low self-esteem will not.

Carroll and Tosi (1970) found in a correlational study that individuals with high self-assurance increased effort in the face of increasingly difficult goals, whereas those with low self-assurance worked less hard as goals became harder. It is likely that different self-perceptions regarding ability underlie the self-assurance measure.

Dossett et al. (1979) found that word processing operators with high self-esteem who were given performance feedback attained their goals significantly more often than individuals with low self-esteem. These results are consistent with those of Schrauger and Rosenberg (1970), who found that shifts in performance following feedback depend on the self-esteem of the individual. Specifically, high self-esteem people improved their performance more than low self-esteem people following positive feedback; the performance of low self-esteem individuals decreased more than high self-esteem individuals following negative feedback. Thus, high self-esteem individuals are influenced more by positives, whereas low self-esteem people are influenced more by negatives.

These results are congruent with Korman's (1970) thesis, which asserts that individuals are motivated to behave in a manner which is congruent with their self-concept. Thus, people respond more to feedback that agrees with their self-concept, whether it is positive or negative, than they do to feedback that is inconsistent with their self-concept.

Internal Versus External Control. In the study of typists (Latham and Yukl, 1976), belief in internal versus external control was found to have no moderating effect on performance. Dossett et al. (1979) also found no moderating effects for locus of control on job performance appraisal measures or on test performance for word processors. However, Latham and Yukl (1976) found that typists with participatively set goals who were "internals" set more difficult goals than "externals."

Conclusions

The only consistent thing about the studies of individual differences in goal setting is their inconsistency. A number of reasons for this can be offered.

First, the studies were not specifically designed to look for individual difference effects. The very fact that most studies assigned goals to the subjects means that any individual differences that did exist were probably masked by the demand characteristics of the design. When goals are assigned, subjects typically respond to situational demands rather than act in accordance with their own styles and preferences. The best design for revealing individual differences would be one in which there is free (or a considerable amount of) goal choice rather than assigned goals. Note that the personality variables in the goal-setting studies reviewed previously were most likely to emerge in the participative conditions (where the subject has some input into the decision) or in the self-set goal conditions.

Second, most of the individual difference variables included in the studies were not based on any clear theoretical rationale; thus, even when differences were found, they were hard to explain. Perhaps the most theoretically plausible of the variables discussed earlier is that of need for achievement. Need for achievement theory (for instance, McClelland and Winter, 1971) would predict, for example, that people high in need for achievement would (a) choose moderate goals; and (b) work hardest when probabilities of success were moderate, when task performance was in their control, when there was performance feedback, and when intrinsic rather than extrinsic rewards were emphasized. Although there is some support for these predictions in the need for achievement literature, goal-setting studies have not been designed to test them.

The results for self-esteem are also intriguing. This variable seems worthy of further study, since it is logical to expect that one's self-concept would affect the goals one chooses. Self-esteem, of course, must be carefully separated from ability.

Third, there are difficulties with regard to the measures used for assessing personality variables. For example, the personality measures used were not consistent across studies. Steers (1975) used the Gough–Heilbrun Adjective Check List (Gough and Heilbrun, 1965) to measure need for achievement, whereas Latham and Yukl (1976) modified a questionnaire developed by Hermans (1970). Therefore it cannot be determined whether the different results obtained in these two studies were due to differences in the measures or in the population. Further, the reliability and validity of personality measures are often inadequate or not reported. In addition, some personality measures were administered after the experimental manipulations had taken place. This procedure can result in a confounding of responses to the personality measures with the experimental treatment.

Fourth, there may be confounding of individual differences in some studies. To draw firm conclusions regarding an individual difference variable, it must be independent of other individual difference variables of interest. Researchers often do not report the intercorrelations of individual differences, yet they draw conclusions on various individual difference variables obtained from the same sample.

Fifth, many studies report that an individual difference variable correlates with performance for people who score high on that variable but not for those who score low. However, generally no test of significance between the two correlations is reported. To establish a moderating effect, a test of significant differences between correlation coefficients should be made (Zedeck, 1971).

Future research must overcome these difficulties before any clear conclusions can be drawn regarding the role of individual differences in goal setting.

Goal Acceptance, Commitment, and Choice

Goal acceptance and commitment are similar though distinguishable concepts. Goal commitment implies a determination to try for a goal (or to keep trying for a goal), but the source of the goal is not specified. It could be an assigned goal or a participatively set goal or a goal that one set on one's own. Goal acceptance implies that one has agreed to commit oneself to a goal assigned or suggested by another person. Both acceptance and commitment presumably can exist in varying degrees. Since most studies have used assigned goals, the two concepts can often be used interchangeably.

Most recent studies of goal setting have used goals as an independent variable. However, since it is assumed that assigned goals must be accepted before they will affect task performance, it is also relevant to examine the determinants of goal commitment or acceptance. Generally, attempts to measure degree of goal commitment in a manner that will differentiate between experimental treatments and/or relate to task performance have failed. None of the experimental conditions in the studies by Latham and Saari (1979a, 1979b), Latham et al. (1978), Yukl and Latham (1978), or Dossett et al.'s Study 1 (1979) affected self-report measures of goal acceptance. Dossett et al.'s (1979) Study 2 found an initial difference, with assigned goals showing greater acceptance than participatively set goals, a prediction contrary to expectations. However, this difference disappeared by the end of the experiment. Frost and Mahoney (1976), London and Oldham (1976), Mento et al. (1980, two studies), Oldham (1975), and Yukl and Latham (1978) found no relationship between measures of goal acceptance and performance. Organ (1977) found that goal acceptance correlated with performance within some of his assigned goal subgroups, but the pattern of correlations was uninterpretable theoretically.

There are several possible reasons for these negative results. First, the measures of goal acceptance (which consisted typically of direct, face-valid questions such as, "How committed are you to attaining the goal?") may not have been valid. Some evidence that the measures of goal acceptance may be at fault was obtained in a study by Hannan (1975) in the credit application evaluation task noted earlier. He measured goal acceptance not by a rating scale but by the degree of difference between the subject's external (assigned or participatively agreed upon) goal and his or her personal goal (as determined from a questionnaire given after external goals were set). Hannan found that participation did lead to greater goal acceptance (though it had no main effect on performance) than assigning goals and that the effects of participation became progressively stronger as the difficulty of the external goal increased. The goal acceptance measure was related to one measure of performance. Hannan also found that personal goals predicted performance better than assigned goals, as did Mento et al. (1980). These findings suggest that indirect measures of goal acceptance may be more valid than direct measures.

Second, in most of the studies where acceptance was measured, nearly all subjects showed complete or substantial goal commitment; thus the range of scores was quite limited. Small differences on the scales typically used may not reflect genuine differences in psychological states.

Third, due to limitations in introspective ability, most (untrained) subjects may not be able to discriminate small differences in psychological commitment (see Nisbett and Wilson, 1977; but see also Lieberman, 1979, for a more sanguine view of the usefulness of introspection). Recall that in the studies by Latham et al. (1978) and Pritchard and Curtis (1973) described earlier, there appeared to be significant commitment effects for monetary incentives based on actual performance, but these were not reflected in the direct goal commitment questions.

The solution to the last two problems may be to modify the design of the typical goal-setting experiment. Designs that encourage a wide range of goal commitment, such as those with a choice of various possible goals, with commitment to each being measured after choice, may reduce the introspective burden and increase the variance of the answers on the commitment scale. Within-subject designs, which involve assigning different goals (under different conditions) to the same subjects at different times, might also make the commitment responses more accurate by providing a clearer frame of reference for the subject. In addition, when a subject is less than fully committed to a given goal, it is important to determine what other goals he or she is committed to. For example, a subject who is not fully committed to a moderately difficult goal could be trying for a harder goal, an easier goal, or no specific goal. Each alternative choice would have different implications for performance.

Different degrees of goal commitment might be induced by varying types or degrees of social influence (for instance, approval, disapproval). Such influences undoubtedly have profound effects on goal choice and commitment among certain individuals, but a detailed discussion of the social-psychological literature is outside the scope of this review.

Goal acceptance or commitment can be considered a form of choice, (the choice between accepting or rejecting a goal that was assigned or set participatively). In this sense these studies tie in with the more traditional studies of what is called "level of aspiration," which allowed subjects freely to choose their own goals after each of a series of trials on a task (for instance, see Frank, 1941; Hilgard, 1958). The factors that affect goal acceptance and goal choice are basically the same. They fit easily into two major categories, which are the main components of expectancy theory (Vroom, 1964).

Expectations of Success

Other things being equal, individuals are more likely to accept or choose a given goal when they have high rather than low expectations of reaching it (Mento et al., 1980). Such expectations evidently stem from self-perceptions about abilty on the task in question (Mento et al., 1980). Presumably these perceptions are inferences from past performance. Past performance has consistently been found to predict future goals (Cummings et al., 1971; Lopes, 1976; Wilsted and Hand, 1974; Ashworth and Mobley[4]). Individuals are more likely to become more confident and to set higher goals after success and to become less confident and to set lower goals after failure (Lewin, 1958), although failure may lead to higher goals in pressure situations (Forward and Zander, 1971; Zander, Forward, and Albert, 1969) or even due to self-induced pressure (Hilgard, 1958). Generalized self-confidence may also affect goal acceptance and choice.

Values

When the perceived value of attaining or trying for a goal is higher, the goal is more likely to be accepted than when the perceived value is low (Mento et al., 1980). The valued outcomes involved may range from intrinsic rewards like the pleasure of achievement to extrinsic rewards following performance, such as money, recognition, and promotion. Instrumentality in expectancy theory is the belief that goal acceptance or goal attainment will lead to value attainment. Theoretically, goal choice and goal acceptance should be predictable from the expectancies, values, and instrumentalities the subject holds with regard to the various choices (Dachler and Mobley, 1973).

This is clearly a maximization-of-satisfaction model, which is not without its critics (for example, Locke, 1975). Nevertheless, treating expectancy theory concepts as factors that predict an individual's goal choices does suggest a way of integrating the expectancy and goal-setting literatures (Dachler and Mobley, 1973; Mento et al., 1980).

Although external factors such as rewards and pressures presumably affect the individual through their effects on expectancies, instrumentalities, and values, it is worth emphasizing *pressures* because they have played a major role in most of the goal-setting studies. For example, the typical laboratory goal-setting study simply involves asking the subject to try to reach a certain goal. The subject typically complies because of the demand characteristics of the experiment (probably reducible to beliefs regarding the value of extra credit and the desire to help the experimenter).

Similarly, in field settings subjects are typically asked to try for goals by their supervisor. The supervisor, of course, is in a position to reward or punish the employee; furthermore, employees know they are being paid to do what the organization asks them to do. Ronan, Latham, and Kinne (1973) found that goal setting among woods workers was only effective when the supervisor stayed on the job with the employees. The mere presence of the supervisor could be considered a form of pressure in this context. In the studies by Forward and Zander (1971) and Zander et al. (1969), competitive or community pressures led to setting goals that were unrealistically high.

Although pressure is something that social scientists generally have been against, Hall and Lawler (1971) argued that if used appropriately (for example, by combining it with responsibility), it can facilitate both high commitment and high performance. Pressure, of course, also can be self-imposed as in the case of the Type A personality who appears to be a compulsive goal achiever (Friedman and Rosenman, 1974).

Summary, Conclusions, and Directions for Future Research

Based on the findings to date, the following conclusions about goal setting seem warranted:

The beneficial effect of goal setting on task performance is one of the most robust and replicable findings in the psychological literature. Ninety percent of the studies showed positive or partially positive effects. Furthermore, these effects are found just as reliably in field settings as in the laboratory.

There are at least four mechanisms by which goals affect task performance: by directing attention and action, mobilizing energy expenditure or effort, prolonging effort over time (persistence), and motivating the individual to develop relevant strategies for goal attainment. The latter two mechanisms are most in need of further study.

Goals are most likely to affect performance under the following conditions:

Range and Type of Goals

Individuals with specific and hard or challenging goals outperform individuals with specific easy goals, do-best goals, or no assigned goals. People with specific moderate goals show performance levels between those of people with easy and hard goals but may not perform better than individuals with do-best goals. A common problem with easy-goal subjects is that their goals are so easy that once they are reached, they set new, higher goals to have something to do, which means that they are no longer genuine easy-goal subjects. Perhaps easy-goal subjects should be told not to try to exceed their goals or not to set new goals when the easy goals are reached.

The wider the range of goal difficulty, the more likely goal setting is to affect performance (cf., Frost and Mahoney, 1976, with Locke et al., 1978). It is probable that longer time spans will progressively increase the difference between subjects with hard goals and those without hard goals.

One aspect of goal setting that has not received much attention to date is the usefulness of setting intermediate goals or subgoals as an aid to attaining longer term or end goals. Locke and Bryan (1967) found that on a two-hour addition task, setting fifteen-minute subgoals led to slightly poorer performance than setting just end goals. Bandura and Simon (1977), however, found that setting weekly goals for weight loss only led to weight loss when daily goals (or multiple goals within days) were set as well. There is probably an optimal time span for the setting of goals depending on both the individual and the task situation. Subgoals could conceivably facilitate performance by operating as a feedback device; they might also serve to maintain effort over long time spans. On the negative side, they might limit performance if the subgoals were treated as performance ceilings. More studies are clearly needed on this topic.

Goal Specificity

Goals seem to regulate performance most predictably when they are expressed in specific quantitative terms (or as specific intentions to take a certain action, such as quitting a job) rather than as vague intentions to "try hard" or as subjective estimates of task or goal difficulty.

Ability

Individuals must have the ability to attain or at least approach their goals. (In complex tasks they must choose appropriate strategies, as noted previously.) Exerting more effort will not improve task performance if improvement is totally beyond the individual's capacity. Goal-setting studies should carefully control for ability (such as by a work sample pretest) to isolate the variance in performance due to goals from that due to ability. If ability is not controlled, it becomes error variance when testing for a motivation effect. The most practical way to set goals may be to base them on each individual's ability on the task in question as measured by a preexperimental work sample. This usually insures ready goal acceptance and makes it easy to control for ability when comparing different goals.

Knowledge of Results (Feedback)

Knowledge of performance in relation to the goal appears to be necessary if goals are to improve performance, just as goals are necessary if feedback is to improve performance. Feedback is probably most helpful as an adjunct to goal setting when the task is divided into trials and feedback is provided after each one, although the ideal frequency is not known. Feedforward, telling the subjects how fast they will need to work on a future trial as compared with their speed on an immediately preceding trial may be a partial substitute in some cases (for instance, see Mento et al., 1980, Study 1). Knowledge and feedback, of course, may have purely cognitive (learning) effects on performance (see Locke et al., 1968, for a discussion of this issue), but these are not the concern of this review. Clearly more research is needed on feedback, especially research based on the issues raised by Ilgen et al. (1979), such as timing, frequency, source, interpretation, and so on.

Monetary Rewards

Money may be an effective method of improving performance in relation to a given goal (presumably through increased commitment), but the amounts involved must be large rather than small (for instance, $3 rather than 3¢ in a typical laboratory experiment).

Further research on money and goal setting could be tied into Deci's work on intrinsic and extrinsic motivation. Deci and Porac (1978) suggested that money rewards that encourage the attainment of competence on a task (reaching a challenging goal?) may enhance rather than decrease interest in the task.

Participation and Supportiveness

There is no consistent evidence that participation in setting goals leads to greater goal commitment or better task performance than assigned goals when goal level is controlled, though it sometimes leads to setting higher goals than the supervisor would have assigned. One study found that participation facilitated the acceptance of hard goals (Hannan, 1975).

Supportiveness may be more important than participation, although this concept needs to be defined more clearly. Latham and Saari (1979b) defined it as friendliness, listening to subjects' opinions about the goal, encouraging questions, and asking rather than telling the subject what to do. More exploration of the nature and effects of supportiveness in goal setting is clearly warranted.

Individual Differences

No reliable individual difference factors (other than ability) have emerged in the goal-setting literature, probably because most of the studies have used assigned goals. Thus, situational constraints have prevented personal styles and preferences from affecting performance. In free-choice situations individual personality traits may play a more substantial role. Subjects high in need for achievement should prefer to set moderate goals, whereas those low in this motive should be more likely to set easy or very hard goals. Individuals with high self-esteem should be more likely to accept and try for challenging goals than those with low self-esteem. However, it is not clear whether a generalized self-esteem measure would show as great an effect as a more task-specific measure of perceived competence. Mento et al. (1980; based on Motowidlo, 1976) found that self-perception of ability added unique variance to performance even when expectancy, valence, and goal level were controlled.

Goal Acceptance and Choice

A basic assumption of goal setting research is that the individual accepts (is actually trying for) the goal that was assigned or was set. Personal goals usually predict performance better than related measures such as assigned (or objective) goal difficulty or subjective goal difficulty. Direct measures of goal acceptance have been found to be generally unrelated to either experimental treatments or task performance. For example, rewards such as money may affect performance, with goal difficulty controlled, even though goal acceptance questions do not indicate increased commitment. Indirect measures, such as the difference between the personal and the assigned goal, show more promise. However, better experimental designs (for example, within-subject designs and designs allowing free choice of goals) may show effects even using direct questions.

Goal choice and acceptance are influenced by numerous factors, including pressure, all of which may work through influencing the individual's expectancies, values, and perceived instrumentalities. Support on the part of higher management for goal-setting programs in organizations seems critical for their success, as is the case for most social science interventions (for example, see Hinrichs, 1978; Ivancevich, 1974; Woodward, Koss, and Hatry[8]). In an organizational context support may include insuring or securing the commitment of middle and lower managers. It is likely that the degree of continuing support for goal-setting programs will determine the duration of their effects. The Latham and Baldes (1975) study with truck drivers has continued to be successful for the past seven years (reported in Latham and Locke, 1979, Figure 1, Footnote b).

Other Issues

Not mentioned in the above discussion was how the type of task affects goal-setting effectiveness. Obviously, individuals must have some control over task pace, quality, method, and so on for goal setting, or any other motivational technique, to affect performance. We do not agree with those who claim that goal setting might work only on certain types of tasks. However, it will undoubtedly be the case that the four mechanisms noted earlier are differentially important in different tasks. For example, where more effort leads to immediate results, goals may work as long as they lead the subject to work harder. On the other hand, where the task is complex, hard goals may only improve performance if they lead to effective strategies.

Regarding the relation of goals to rewards, an intriguing finding by Masters et al. (1977) was that children who were told to evaluate their performance after each trial block while speaking into a tape recorder (for example, "I did very good [sic];" "I didn't do very good [sic]") all reached assymptote on the task regardless of their assigned goals. Self-reward ultimately vitiated what had been highly significant goal effects. This finding is clearly worthy of future study.

Competition in relation to goal setting also requires further study. Both Latham and Baldes (1975) and Komaki et al. (1978) found that goal setting plus feedback led to spontaneous competition among subjects. White et al. (1977) found that telling subjects that their performance would be compared to that of others ("evaluation apprehension," in their terminology) had a powerful effect on task performance independent of a separate goal manipulation. However, spontaneous goal setting within the evaluation apprehension condition was not measured. It is likely that competition could lead people to set higher goals than they would otherwise (other people's performances become the goals) and/or lead to greater goal commitment (Locke, 1968).

Another issue that has not been investigated is whether hard goals combined with high pressure might lead to a conflict situation and therefore high anxiety. It has been shown that anxiety disrupts performance on complex tasks when it leads subjects to worry rather than concentrate on the task (Wine, 1971). As noted earlier, conflicts may also occur among different goals, although this has not been studied. Conflicting pressures in goal setting may vitiate the usual goal–performance relationship (Forward and Zander, 1971). Nor has the issue of individual versus group goal setting received much attention. (Group goals are discussed in Zander, 1971.)

A final note is in order with respect to the practical significance of the technique of goal setting. In a review of all available experimental field studies of goal setting, Locke et al. (1980) found that the median improvement in performance (for instance, productivity, quality) that resulted from goal setting was 16 percent. In one company the use of goal setting on just one job saved a company $250,000 (Latham and Baldes, 1975). Combined with the use of monetary incentives, Locke et al. (1980) found that goal setting improved performance by a median of more than 40 percent—a finding of great practical significance.

A model for the use of goal setting in field settings has been developed by Latham and Locke (1979). White and Locke (in press) have documented the high frequency with which goals actually regulate productivity in business settings. Locke (1978) has argued that goal setting is recognized explicitly or implicitly in virtually every theory of and approach to work motivation.

Notes

1. Our view of what constitutes a goal attribute differs from that of Steers and Porter (1974) who, for example, called participation an attribute of goals. We treat participation as a mechanism that may *affect* goal content or goal acceptance.

2. Shapira, Z. *Goal difficulty and goal setting as determinants of task motivation.* Unpublished manuscript, Hebrew University, 1977.

3. Partially or conditionally supportive studies were distinguished from nonsupportive studies as follows: A study was called partially supportive if the treatment was significant for one subsample of the full sample of subjects or for one of several experimental treatments or criteria. If an entire sample or study found no significant effects, it was called nonsupportive.

4. Ashworth, D.N., and Mobley, W.H. *Relationships among organizational entry performance goals, subsequent goals, and performance in a military setting* (Tech. Rep. TR-6). Columbia: Center for Management and Organizational Research, University of South Carolina, July 1978.

5. Dockstader, S.L. *Performance standards and implicit goal setting: Field testing Locke's assumption.* Paper presented at the meeting of the American Psychological Association, San Francisco, August 1977.

6. Saari, L.M., and Latham, G.P. *Hypotheses on reinforcing properties of incentives contingent upon performance.* Unpublished manuscript, University of Washington, 1980.

7. Likert, R. Personal communication, August 1977.

8. Woodward, J.P., Koss, M.P., and Hatry, H.P. *Performance targeting in local government: An examination of current usage, impacts, and implementation factors.* Washington, D.C.: Urban Institute, 1978.

References

Adam, E.E. Behavior modification in quality control. *Academy of Management Journal,* 1975, *18,* 662–679.

Andrews, F.M., and Farris, G.F. Time pressure and performance of scientists and engineers: A five-year panel study. *Organizational Behavior and Human Performance,* 1972, *8,* 185–200.

Annett, J. *Feedback and human behaviour.* Baltimore, Md.: Penguin Books, 1969.

At Emery Air Freight: Positive reinforcement boosts performance. *Organizational Dynamics,* 1973, *1*(3), 41–50.

Bandura, A. *Social learning theory*. Englewood Cliffs, N.J.: Prentice-Hall, 1977.

Bandura, A., and Simon, K.M. The role of proximal intentions in self-regulation of refractory behavior. *Cognitive Therapy and Research*, 1977, *1*, 177–193.

Bassett, G.A. A study of the effects of task goal and schedule choice on work performance. *Organizational Behavior and Human Performance*, 1979, *24*, 202–227.

Bavelas, J.B. Systems analysis of dyadic interaction: Prediction from individual parameters. *Behavioral Science*, 1978, *23*, 177–186.

Bavelas, J.B., and Lee, E.S. Effects of goal level on performance: A trade-off of quantity and quality. *Canadian Journal of Psychology*, 1978, *32*(4), 219–240.

Becker, L.J. Joint effect of feedback and goal setting on performance: A field study of residential energy conservation. *Journal of Applied Psychology*, 1978, *63*, 428–433.

Blumenfeld, W.S., and Leidy, T.R. Effectiveness of goal setting as a management device: Research note. *Psychological Reports*, 1969, *24*, 752.

Bragg, J.E., and Andrews, I.R. Participative decision-making: An experimental study in a hospital. *Journal of Applied Behavioral Science*, 1973, *9*, 727–735.

Brass, D.J., and Oldham, G.R. Validating an in-basket test using an alternative set of leadership scoring dimensions. *Journal of Applied Psychology*, 1976, *61*, 652–657.

Burke, R.J., and Wilcox, D.S. Characteristics of effective employee performance review and development interviews. *Personnel Psychology*, 1969, *22*, 291–305.

Campbell, D.J., and Ilgen, D.R. Additive effects of task difficulty and goal setting on subsequent task performance. *Journal of Applied Psychology*, 1976, *61*, 319–324.

Carroll, S.J., Jr., and Tosi, H.L. Goal characteristics and personality factors in a management-by-objectives program. *Administrative Science Quarterly*, 1970, *15*, 295–305.

Christensen-Szalanski, J.J.J. A further examination of the selection of problem-solving strategies: The effects of deadlines and analytic aptitudes. *Organizational Behavior and Human Performance*, 1980, *25*, 107–122.

Chung, K.H., and Vickery, W.D. Relative effectiveness and joint effects of three selected reinforcements in a repetitive task situation. *Organizational Behavior and Human Performance*, 1976, *16*, 114–142.

Cummings, L.L., Schwab, D.P., and Rosen, M. Performance and

knowledge of results as determinants of goal setting. *Journal of Applied Psychology*, 1971, *55*, 526–530.

Dachler, H.P., and Mobley, W.H. Construct validation of an instrumentality-expectancy-task-goal model of work motivation: Some theoretical boundary conditions. *Journal of Applied Psychology*, 1973, *58*, 397–418 (Monograph).

Deci, E.L., and Porac, J. Cognitive evaluation theory and the study of human motivation. In M.R. Lepper and D. Greene (Eds.), *The hidden costs of reward*. Hillsdale, N.J.: Erlbaum, 1978.

Dossett, D.L., Latham, G.P., and Mitchell, T.R. The effects of assigned versus participatively set goals, KR, and individual differences when goal difficulty is held constant. *Journal of Applied Psychology*, 1979, *64*, 291–298.

Erez, M. Feedback: A necessary condition for the goal setting–performance relationship. *Journal of Applied Psychology*, 1977, *62*, 624–627.

Fishbein, M., and Ajzen, I. *Belief, attitude, intention, and behavior: An introduction to theory and research*. Reading, Mass: Addison-Wesley, 1975.

Forward, J., and Zander, A. Choice of unattainable group goals and effects on performance. *Organizational Behavior and Human Performance*, 1971, *6*, 184–199.

Frank, J.D. Recent studies of the level of aspiration. *Psychological Bulletin*, 1941, *38*, 218–226.

French, J.R.P., Kay, E., and Meyer, H.H. Participation and the appraisal system. *Human Relations*, 1966, *19*, 3–20.

Friedman, M., and Rosenman, R.H. *Type A behavior and your heart*. New York: Knopf, 1974.

Frost, P.J., and Mahoney, T.A. Goal setting and the task process: 1. An interactive influence on individual performance. *Organizational Behavior and Human Performance*, 1976, *17*, 328–350.

Gough, H.G., and Heilbrun, A.B. *The Adjective Checklist manual*. Palo Alto, Calif.: Consulting Psychologists Press, 1965.

Greller, M.M. Evaluation of feedback sources as a function of role and organizational level. *Journal of Applied Psychology*, 1980, *65*, 24–27.

Hackman, J.R., and Lawler, E.E. Employee reactions to job characteristics. *Journal of Applied Psychology*, 1971, *55*, 259–286 (Monograph).

Hall, D.T., and Foster, L.W. A psychological success cycle and goal setting: Goals, performance, and attitudes. *Academy of Management Journal*, 1977, *20*, 282–290.

Hall, D.T., and Hall, F.S. The relationship between goals, performance, success, self-image, and involvement under different organizational climates. *Journal of Vocational Behavior,* 1976, *9,* 267–278.

Hall, D.T., and Lawler, E.E. Job pressures and research performance. *American Scientist,* 1971, *59*(1), 64–73.

Hamner, W.C., and Harnett, D.L. Goal-setting, performance and satisfaction in an interdependent task. *Organizational Behavior and Human Performance,* 1974, *12,* 217–230.

Hannan, R.L. *The effects of participation in goal setting on goal acceptance and performance: A laboratory experiment.* Unpublished doctoral dissertation, University of Maryland, 1975.

Hermans, H.J.M. A questionnaire measure of achievement motivation. *Journal of Applied Psychology,* 1970, *54,* 353–363.

Hilgard, E.R. Success in relation to level of aspiration. In C.L. Stacey and M.F. DeMartino (Eds.), *Understanding human motivation.* Cleveland, Ohio: Howard Allen, 1958.

Hinrichs, J.R. *Practical management for productivity.* New York: Van Nostrand Reinhold, 1978.

Ilgen, D.R., Fisher, C.D., and Taylor, M.S. Consequences of individual feedback on behavior in organizations. *Journal of Applied Psychology,* 1979, *64,* 349–371.

Ivancevich, J.M. Changes in performance in a management by objectives program. *Administrative Science Quarterly,* 1974, *19,* 563–574.

————. Effects of goal setting on performance and job satisfaction. *Journal of Applied Psychology,* 1976, *61,* 605–612.

————. Different goal setting treatments and their effects on performance and job satisfaction. *Academy of Management Journal,* 1977, *20,* 406–419.

Ivancevich, J.M., and McMahon, J.T. Black-white differences in a goal-setting program. *Organizational Behavior and Human Performance,* 1977, *20,* 287–300. (a)

————. Education as a moderator of goal setting effectiveness. *Journal of Vocational Behavior,* 1977, *11,* 83–94. (b)

————. A study of task-goal attributes, higher order need strength, and performance. *Academy of Management Journal,* 1977, *20,* 552–563. (c)

Kahneman, D. *Attention and effort.* Englewood Cliffs, N.J.: Prentice-Hall, 1973.

Kaplan, R., and Rothkopf, E.Z. Instructional objectives as directions to learners: Effect of passage length and amount of objective-relevant content. *Journal of Educational Psychology,* 1974, *66,* 448–456.

Kim, J.S., and Hamner, W.C. Effect of performance feedback and goal setting on productivity and satisfaction in an organizational setting. *Journal of Applied Psychology,* 1976, *61,* 48–57.

Kolb, D.A., and Boyatzis, R.E. Goal-setting and self-directed behavior change. *Human Relations,* 1970, *23,* 439–457.

Komaki, J., Barwick, K.D., and Scott, L.R. A behavioral approach to occupational safety: Pinpointing and reinforcing safe performance in a food manufacturing plant. *Journal of Applied Psychology,* 1978, *64,* 434–445.

Korman, A.K. Toward a hypothesis of work behavior. *Journal of Applied Psychology,* 1970, *54,* 31–41.

LaPorte, R.E., and Nath, R. Role of performance goals in prose learning. *Journal of Educational Psychology,* 1976, *68,* 260–264.

Latham, G.P., and Baldes, J.J. The "practical significance" of Locke's theory of goal setting. *Journal of Applied Psychology,* 1975, *60,* 122–124.

Latham, G.P., and Kinne, S.B., III. Improving job performance through training in goal setting. *Journal of Applied Psychology,* 1974, *59,* 187–191.

Latham, G.P., and Locke, E.A. Increasing productivity with decreasing time limits: A field replication of Parkinson's law. *Journal of Applied Psychology,* 1975, *60,* 524–526.

———. Goal-setting: A motivational technique that works. *Organizational Dynamics,* 1979, *8*(2), 68–80.

Latham, G.P., Mitchell, T.R., and Dossett, D.L. Importance of participative goal setting and anticipated rewards on goal difficulty and job performance. *Journal of Applied Psychology,* 1978, *63,* 163–171.

Latham, G.P., and Saari, L.M. The effects of holding goal difficulty constant on assigned and participatively set goals. *Academy of Management Journal,* 1979, *22,* 163–168. (a)

———. Importance of supportive relationships in goal setting. *Journal of Applied Psychology,* 1979, *64,* 151–156. (b)

Latham, G.P., and Yukl, G.A. Assigned versus participative goal setting with educated and uneducated woods workers. *Journal of Applied Psychology,* 1975, *60,* 299–302. (a)

———. A review of research on the application of goal setting in organizations. *Academy of Management Journal,* 1975, *18,* 824–845. (b)

———. Effects of assigned and participative goal setting on performance and job satisfaction. *Journal of Applied Psychology,* 1976, *61,* 166–171.

Lewin, K. Psychology of success and failure. In C.L. Stacey and M.F.

DeMartino (Eds.), *Understanding human motivation.* Cleveland, Ohio: Howard Allen, 1958.

Lieberman, D.A. Behaviorism and the mind: A (limited) call for a return to introspection. *American Psychologist,* 1979, *34,* 319–333.

Locke, E.A. Motivational effects of knowledge of results: Knowledge or goal setting? *Journal of Applied Psychology,* 1967, *51,* 324–329.

———. Toward a theory of task motivation and incentives. *Organizational Behavior and Human Performance,* 1968, *3,* 157–189.

———. Purpose without consciousness: A contradiction. *Psychological Reports,* 1969, *25,* 991–1009.

———. Critical analysis of the concept of causality in behavioristic psychology. *Psychological Reports,* 1972, *31,* 175–197.

———. Personnel attitudes and motivation. *Annual Review of Psychology,* 1975, *26,* 457–480.

———. The myths of behavior mod in organizations. *Academy of Management Review,* 1977, *2,* 543–553.

———. The ubiquity of the technique of goal setting in theories of and approaches to employee motivation. *Academy of Management Review,* 1978, *3,* 594–601.

———. Latham versus Komaki: A tale of two paradigms. *Journal of Applied Psychology,* 1980, *65,* 16–23.

Locke, E.A., and Bryan, J.F. Cognitive aspects of psychomotor performance: The effects of performance goals on level of performance. *Journal of Applied Psychology,* 1966, *50,* 286–291.

———. Performance goals as determinants of level of performance and boredom. *Journal of Applied Psychology,* 1967, *51,* 120–130.

———. Goal-setting as a determinant of the effect of knowledge of score on performance. *American Journal of Psychology,* 1968, *81,* 398–406.

———. The directing function of goals in task performance. *Organizational Behavior and Human Performance,* 1969, *4,* 35–42. (a)

———. Knowledge of score and goal level as determinants of work rate. *Journal of Applied Psychology,* 1969, *53,* 59–65. (b)

Locke, E.A., Bryan, J.F., and Kendall, L.M. Goals and intentions as mediators of the effects of monetary incentives on behavior. *Journal of Applied Psychology,* 1968, *52,* 104–121.

Locke, E.A., Cartledge, N., and Knerr, C.S. Studies of the relationship between satisfaction, goal setting, and performance. *Organizational Behavior and Human Performance.* 1970, *5,* 135–158.

Locke, E.A., Cartledge, N., and Koeppel, J. Motivational effects of knowledge of results: A goal-setting phenomenon? *Psychological Bulletin,* 1968, *70,* 474–485.

Locke, E.A., Feren, D.B., McCaleb, V.M., Shaw, K.N., and Denny,

A.T. The relative effectiveness of four methods of motivating employee performance. In K. Duncan, M. Gruneberg, and D. Wallis (Eds.), *Changes in working life.* New York: Wiley, 1980.

Locke, E.A., Mento, A.J., and Katcher, B.L. The interaction of ability and motivation in performance: An exploration of the meaning of moderators. *Personnel Psychology,* 1978, *31,* 269–280.

Locke, E.A., and Schweiger, D.M. Participation in decision-making: One more look. In B.M. Staw (Ed.), *Research in organizational behavior* (Vol. 1). Greenwich, Conn.: JAI Press, 1979.

London, M., and Oldham, G.R. Effects of varying goal types and incentive systems on performance and satisfaction. *Academy of Management Journal,* 1976, *19,* 537–546.

Lopes, L.L. Individual strategies in goal-setting. *Organizational Behavior and Human Performance,* 1976, *15,* 268–277.

Masters, J.C., Furman, W., and Barden, R.C. Effects of achievement standards, tangible rewards, and self-dispensed achievement evaluations on children's task mastery. *Child Development,* 1977, *48,* 217–224.

McClelland, D.C., and Winter, D.G. *Motivating economic achievement.* New York: Free Press, 1971.

Meichenbaum, D. *Cognitive-behavior modification.* New York: Plenum Press, 1977.

Mento, A.J., Cartledge, N.D., and Locke, E.A. Maryland vs. Michigan vs. Minnesota: Another look at the relationship of expectancy and goal difficulty to task performance. *Organizational Behavior and Human Performance,* 1980, *25,* 419–440.

Migliore, R.H. *MBO: Blue collar to top executive.* Washington, D.C.: Bureau of National Affairs, 1977.

Miller, G.A., Galanter, E., and Pribram, K.H. *Plans and the structure of behavior.* New York: Holt, 1960.

Miller, H.E., Katerberg, R., and Hulin, C.L. Evaluation of the Mobley, Horner, and Hollingsworth model of employee turnover. *Journal of Applied Psychology,* 1979, *64,* 509–517.

Mobley, W.H., Horner, S.O., and Hollingsworth, A.T. An evaluation of precursors of hospital employee turnover. *Journal of Applied Psychology,* 1978, *63,* 408–414.

Mobley, W.H., Hand, H.H., Baker, R.L., and Meglino, B.M. Conceptual and empirical analysis of military recruit training attrition. *Journal of Applied Psychology,* 1979, *64,* 10–18.

Mossholder, K.W. Effects of externally mediated goal setting on intrinsic motivation: A laboratory experiment. *Journal of Applied Psychology,* 1980, *65,* 202–210.

Motowidlo, S.J. *A laboratory study of the effects of situational char-*

acteristics and individual differences on task success and motivation to perform a numerical task. Unpublished doctoral dissertation, University of Minnesota, 1976.

Motowidlo, S., Loehr, V., and Dunnette, M.D. A laboratory study of the effects of goal specificity on the relationship between probability of success and performance. *Journal of Applied Psychology,* 1978, *63,* 172–179.

Nemeroff, W.F., and Cosentino, J. Utilizing feedback and goal setting to increase performance appraisal interviewer skills of managers. *Academy of Management Journal,* 1979, *22,* 566–576.

Ness, R.G., and Patton, R.W. The effect of beliefs on maximum weight-lifting performance. *Cognitive Therapy and Research,* 1979, *3,* 205–211.

Nisbett, R.E., and Wilson, T.D. Telling more than we can know: Verbal reports on mental processes. *Psychological Review,* 1977, *84,* 231–259.

Odiorne, G.S. MBO: A backward glance. *Business Horizons,* October 1978, pp. 14–24.

Oldham, G.R. The impact of supervisory characteristics on goal acceptance. *Academy of Management Journal,* 1975, *18,* 461–475.

———. The motivational strategies used by supervisors: Relationships to effectiveness indicators. *Organizational Behavior and Human Performance,* 1976, *15,* 66–86.

Organ, D.W. Intentional vs arousal effects of goal-setting. *Organizational Behavior and Human Performance,* 1977, *18,* 378–389.

Pritchard, R.D., and Curtis, M.I. The influence of goal setting and financial incentives on task performance. *Organizational Behavior and Human Performance,* 1973, *10,* 175–183.

Rand. A. *Introduction to objectivist epistemology.* New York: The Objectivist, 1967.

Reynolds, R.E., Standiford, S.N., and Anderson, R.C. Distribution of reading time when questions are asked about a restricted category of text information. *Journal of Educational Psychology,* 1979, *71,* 183–190.

Ronan, W.W., Latham, G.P., and Kinne, S.B., III. Effects of goal setting and supervision on worker behavior in an industrial situation. *Journal of Applied Psychology,* 1973, *58,* 302–307.

Rosswork, S.G. Goal setting: The effects on an academic task with varying magnitudes of incentive. *Journal of Educational Psychology,* 1977, *69,* 710–715.

Rothkopf, E.Z., and Billington, M.J. A two-factor model of the effect of goal-descriptive directions on learning from text. *Journal of Educational Psychology,* 1975, *67,* 692–704.

————. Goal-guided learning from text: Inferring a descriptive processing model from inspection times and eye movements. *Journal of Educational Psychology*, 1979, *71*, 310–327.

Rothkopf, E.Z., and Kaplan, R. Exploration of the effect of density and specificity of instructional objectives on learning from text. *Journal of Educational Psychology*, 1972, *63*, 295–302.

Ryan, T.A. *Intentional behavior: An approach to human motivation*. New York: Ronald Press, 1970.

Sales, S.M. Some effects of role overload and role underload. *Organizational Behavior and Human Performance*, 1970, *5*, 592–608.

Schrauger, J.S., and Rosenberg, S.F. Self-esteem and the effects of success and failure feedback on performance. *Journal of Personality*, 1970, *38*, 404–417.

Searfoss, D.G., and Monczka, R.M. Perceived participation in the budget process and motivation to achieve the budget. *Academy of Management Journal*, 1973, *16*, 541–554.

Singh, J.P. *Some personality moderators of the effects of repeated success and failure on task-related variables*. Unpublished doctoral dissertation, University of Akron, 1972.

Steers, R.M. Task-goal attributes, n achievement, and supervisory performance. *Organizational Behavior and Human Performance*, 1975, *13*, 392–403.

Steers, R.M., and Porter, L.W. The role of task-goal attributes in employee performance. *Psychological Bulletin*, 1974, *81*, 434–452.

Strang, H.R., Lawrence, E.C. and Fowler, P.C. Effects of assigned goal level and knowledge of results on arithmetic computation: A laboratory study. *Journal of Applied Psychology*, 1978, *63*, 446–450.

Taylor, F.W. *The principles of scientific management*. New York: Norton, 1967. (Originally published, 1911.)

Terborg, J.R. The motivational components of goal setting. *Journal of Applied Psychology*, 1976, *61*, 613–621.

Terborg, J.R., and Miller, H.E. Motivation, behavior, and performance: A closer examination of goal setting and monetary incentives. *Journal of Applied Psychology*, 1978, *63*, 29–39.

Umstot, D.D., Bell, C.H., Jr., and Mitchell, T.R. Effects of job enrichment and task goals on satisfaction and productivity: Implications for job design. *Journal of Applied Psychology*, 1976, *61*, 379–394.

Vroom, V. *Work and motivation*. New York: Wiley, 1964.

Wexley, K.N., and Nemeroff, W.F. Effectiveness of positive reinforcement and goal setting as methods of management development. *Journal of Applied Psychology*, 1975, *60*, 446–450.

White, F.M., and Locke, E.A. Perceived determinants of high and low productivity in three occupational groups: A critical incident study. *Journal of Management Studies*, in press.

White, S.E., Mitchell, T.R., and Bell, C.H., Jr. Goal setting, evaluation apprehension, and social cues as determinants of job performance and job satisfaction in a simulated organization. *Journal of Applied Psychology*, 1977, *62*, 665–673.

Wilsted, W.D., and Hand, H.H. Determinants of aspiration levels in a simulated goal setting environment of the firm. *Academy of Management Journal*, 1974, *17*, 172–177.

Wine, J. Test anxiety and direction of attention. *Psychological Bulletin*, 1971, *76*, 92–104.

Yates, J.F., and Kulick, R.M. Effort control and judgments. *Organizational Behavior and Human Performance*, 1977, *20*, 54–65.

Yukl, G.A., and Latham, G.P. Interrelationships among employee participation, individual differences, goal difficulty, goal acceptance, goal instrumentality, and performance. *Personnel Psychology*, 1978, *31*, 305–323.

Zander, A. *Motives and goals in groups*. New York: Academic Press, 1971.

Zander, A., Forward, J., and Albert, R. Adaptation of board members to repeated failure or success by their organization. *Organizational Behavior and Human Performance*, 1969, *4*, 56–76.

Zedeck, S. Problems with the use of "moderator" variables. *Psychological Bulletin*, 1971, *76*, 295–310.

3

Performance Assessment and Retail Organizational Effectiveness

Richard Klimoski

The premise of this chapter is that performance assessment systems in organizations are a key to human resources management. That is, they should be at the center of efforts to bring about an effective organization, one that will compete well in the turbulent business environment of this decade.

What Are Performance Assessment Systems?

To give you my orientation, performance assessment systems include those activities associated with defining and measuring an employee's contribution to an organization. The phrase refers to the various procedures and techniques that index a person's effectiveness. Performance assessment systems also include the way data on the effectiveness of specific individuals or groups of individuals are actually used, for example, for developing and shaping personnel policy, for maintaining control, and for bringing about enhanced capabilities on the part of the people employed by an organization.

We normally think about performance assessment in terms of its potential effects on the individual being evaluated, since carrying out assessments is frequently tied to administrative decisions regarding employees. Thus, in many organizations, decisions with regard to making changes in compensation, establishing likelihood of promotion, or ranking of employees at a time when reduction in force is warranted are based on assessed levels of effectiveness. Similarly, evaluations are often used as the basis for efforts to increase an employee's lagging motivation or to identify particular areas that need remediation through coaching or training. Here the assessment of weaknesses becomes especially relevant. We traditionally think of performance assessment systems as implying administrative and developmental actions directed toward specific employees.

67

The Importance of Performance Assessment Systems

The procedures used and data generated in such assessment programs can have useful application to broader concerns of organizational management. To illustrate, most theories of effective management planning and control stress the importance of the establishment of corporate goals and objectives. These goals and objectives usually derive from the mission of the organization as assumed by its senior management and are framed in terms that make sense in light of present and future competition and anticipated developments. Moreover, as usually formulated, these goals and objectives constitute future, anticipated, or desired states against which progress or corporate success can be determined. As a character in *Alice in Wonderland* asks if you do not know where you are going, how can you tell if you get there?

But back to the point at hand. For these goals or objectives to direct and shape the activities of managers and employees alike, they need to be elaborated on or fleshed out in terms that make sense for the individual. Performance assessment systems constitute the single most effective technique for doing this.

This assertion stems from the logic and procedures of performance assessment programs. As a starting point, they rely on management's definition of the areas of responsibility to be given to an employee and on the goals or objectives to be set in those responsibility areas. Thus, in the course of development of assessment parameters, a great deal of consideration can be given to how the job of a particular employee fits into or relates to the work to be performed by others. Moreover, at the same time, the goals and objectives toward which the employee is working can be made consistent with those established for the department, the division, or the corporate whole. Clearly, care in the establishment of the parameters for assessment (or criteria for effectiveness) can pay off in bringing about a coherence to the efforts of all those involved working for an organization. It can help to insure that the energies expended by all individuals in various departments or groups are synchronized and result in synergy rather than syncopation.

What Do We Assess?

When it comes to evaluating individuals, whether they be senior management, first-level supervisors, or hourly employees, we have had three general options when it comes to the content of assessments. Historically, assessments or evaluations have frequently focused on the personal traits or qualities of an individual. That is to say, when we have defined effectiveness we have thought in terms of those traits that seemed important to performing the job in question. Traits like initiative, dependability, and loyalty frequently come to mind. An effective employee has these traits. Performance results is a second area that could be used in defining what constitutes effectiveness in employees. Results may be couched in terms of such indicators as "sales made per square foot of space," market share, employee turnover rate, or consumer awareness ratings; these are regularly used as indexes. More recently, a third option has enjoyed support among managers and consultants. This is an emphasis on behavior. In this framework one can evaluate a person's effectiveness in terms of behaviors exhibited on the job. To restate the distinction, the trait approach emphasizes what a person is, the behavior approach stresses what a person does, and the results approach focuses on what are presumed to be the products of a person's efforts and behaviors.

An illustration might be in order. Consider an assistant manager in a retail store. If I were to assess his or her effectiveness, I could rely on my observations of the results produced. For example, an assistant manager's effectiveness might be related to the frequency with which shelves are noted to be poorly stocked. Or I could assess effectiveness in terms of behaviors such as the manager's checking on displays, ordering items or even his or her keeping adequate inventories of popular products. Finally, I could beg the question of specific outcomes or behaviors and assess the manager in terms of traits. I might directly ask for or make assessment of his or her levels of conscientiousness or foresight.

As it turns out, each of these approaches to defining (referencing) effectiveness has strengths and weaknesses. Each is more or less applicable to particular jobs, to types of industries, and to differing management philosophies. Each one will be more or less appropriate depending on the purpose of the assessment. For example, a results approach might be more suitable as a basis for awarding a bonus. A behavior emphasis would be better when assessments are to be used to determine a manager's training needs. A person or trait orientation makes sense when the assessment is to be used as input to making a promotion decision. In this last case, we need to predict a person's likely future success, and knowing his or her personal traits or qualities helps us to do this.

Regardless of the differential strengths and weaknesses of each approach to assessment, they share a major attribute. They usually contain a subjective element; they require human judgment. That is to say, at some point an individual or group must render an opinion about the person's effectiveness. Even results-oriented assessment programs require judgment calls in determining the degree to which objectives have been met, in interpreting results relative to constraints or contingencies, and in addressing qualitative aspects of performance. It seems very clear that subjectivity enters into the assessment of traits or the indexing of the frequency of demonstration of key behaviors.

Thus, for better or worse, we must acknowledge the importance of judgment in most appraisal contexts. Fortunately, it turns out that we know a fair amount about the subjective elements in assessments. The key is to make use of this knowledge in developing and implementing assessment systems in organizations.

Promoting Quality Assessments

Three conditions are known to influence strongly the quality of assessments. When laid out directly, they appear rather straightforward or intuitive. But as it turns out, as obvious as they seem, organizational policymakers frequently ignore them, or worse still, through the decisions that they make they set up dynamics that frequently work to frustrate their purpose.

The first condition relates to the need for assessments to be based on frequent and appropriate observations. Simply stated, the quality or validity of an evaluation is strongly affected by the amount of contact a supervisor has with his or her subordinates. This does seem straightforward, yet this principle is frequently violated, as in the case when we have middle managers evaluating hourly employees or corporate personnel assessing field staff. The nature and frequency of contact required will depend somewhat on the job involved. But as a general rule, more is better.

We normally assume that a person's immediate supervisor is in an excellent position to evaluate a person because he or she has regular and frequent contact with the focal employee. We also assume that the supervisor also meets a second requirement: the capability to evaluate accurately. This capability is based on a good knowledge of the work to be performed by a subordinate and a clear idea of what constitutes good performance. But capability also means a reasonable mastery of the evaluation system, the rating scales, the method of recordiing and documenting assessments and recommendations, and so on. Capability also includes being able to interpret and make use of performance assessment data produced by other people. How many persons responsible for performance reviews in your organization can be said to meet this second condition?

The third condition is somewhat harder to characterize, but essentially it refers to the motivation to evaluate people accurately. Evaluations that are based on frequent observations or contact, that are performed by someone who has been trained, will still be worthless if he or she is not motivated to conscientious effort. Both the technical and popular literature are full of examples where a carefully designed system fails to fulfill its promise because of reluctant participation and lack of effort by managers. Frequently, not only is there a lack of incentive to do an accurate job but also, at times, there are organizational forces conspiring to present a specific bias in evaluations, as in the case of what has been called the error of leniency. While opportunity to observe can be insured by careful selection of who will be doing the assessments, and capability can be dramatically enhanced through training programs, it is this last condition that is hardest to meet. In most organizations, where performance assessment systems fail, it is because the managers who are responsible lack the motivation to perform them carefully or to even perform them at all.

The Challenge: Motivating Careful Assessment

If quality performance assessments are a goal, there are several things that must be attended to. Some of these can be thought of as preconditions and others are more directly tied to the issue of motivation just raised.

It seems clear that performance assessment can be carried out only in a context where some thought has been given to the relationship of each manager's or employee's job to corporate goals and objectives. The areas of responsibility identified for an employee must be consistent with the kind of contribution that that person must make relative to the efforts of others. This places a fair burden on top management to articulate the linkages of each level and each position to immediate, intermediate, and long-term objectives. You have to be sure that what you are assessing is relevant.

Frequently, this requires effort directed in a systematic process of what has been called means/ends analysis. The goals of a particular division or department must be tied to the larger corporate objective. And, in turn, each manager in that unit should be held accountable for performing those behaviors or producing those products that are likely to insure that the subunit meets these goals.

The issue of training has been raised already. But it deserves repeating. A precondition for quality assessments is that managers at all levels be skilled in the application and use of the assessment system.

This usually means that efficient training programs must be designed and that managers be expected to attend them.

These preconditions notwithstanding, ultimately the critical issue of motivation toward accuracy must be confronted. But, in my opinion, it can only be dealt with by creating a climate or ethic for careful and considered employee assessment. I also feel that prime responsibility for doing this lies with upper management, and especially with the chief executive officer. Based on this assumption, here are some things that must be done to create this climate:

Top management must establish and support specialists within the organization itself who are capable of developing and implementing appraisal systems. Consultants can help. But one needs to have some element of advocacy for quality performance assessment on a continuing and regular basis. A competent and professional staff can do this.

Top management must personally use and demonstrate careful assessment of its own staff. Actions speak louder than words. A climate for careful assessment can be strengthened by having senior managers experience the reality and the benefits of same, in the role of subordinates to the top managers. The format might be different. The frequency of review might be different. But the dynamics set up by the careful review of performance, say, by the CEO and his or her staff, will be the same. In my judgment, a careful review can have consequences as positive as if it had occurred at the lowest levels of the corporate ladder.

Careful performance assessment should be made an explicit part of each manager's job responsibility. It may even be written into a job description (as is already frequently done). In any event, holding a manager accountable for regular and effective performance reviews with his or her own subordinates will go a long way toward creating the climate envisioned. When that manager realizes that his or her future advancement depends, in part, on skill and effectiveness in the appraisal area, we will see much more effort expended in this direction. It must become an expectation on the part of managers at all levels.

Make use of appraisal data in corporate decisions affecting staffing. Numerous corporate decisions are made that affect the present and future status of personnel. Appraisal data should be gathered and incorporated in management information systems. And most importantly, it should be used. Decisions with regard to promotions, to reductions in force, or to salary adjustments should be based, at least in part, on assessed performance. Nothing is as likely to cause managers to treat the assessment process seriously as a belief that it is an activity that really counts. When coupled with some of the other recommendations made above, this seriousness of purpose can result in greater quality. But the converse is also true. If assessments and resulting data are *not* used as input to important decisions, there is an equally high probability that effort at carrying out assessments will sink to low levels.

Conclusions

We are told that the 1980s will be the decade where productivity is the watchword. Many people have raised concerns in this area, and numerous programs have been developed to ameliorate what some people are describing as a battle for economic survival in a global marketplace. It is my belief that a reaffirmation of the importance of systematic performance assessment will go a long way in creating the needed competitive edge. A continuing commitment to effectiveness (and to excellence) must be rooted in the regular expectations of effectiveness that can only be set up and promoted by a well designed performance assessment program. But the key is a senior management group that takes an active role in seeing to it that such a system remains viable over the long term.

4

Performance Appraisal: An Update

Kenneth N. Wexley and
Richard Klimoski

One of the oldest areas of concern to Industrial/Organizational psychologists and personnel specialists is currently one of the most active in terms of research, theory building and practice. Performance Appraisal—the process by which employees are assessed for purposes of enhancing their development or formulating an administrative decision—is a topic that appears to have become a major theme for the 1980s.

Traditionally, the I/O psychologist's involvement in performance evaluation stemmed from his or her competency in psychometrics on the one hand, and individual assessment on the other. The former influence has been particularly great over the years as reflected in the numerous and sophisticated scales or sytems of measurement produced. Indeed, to many, performance appraisal *was* the scale or technique for measurement used in an organization. In fact, attention to good measurement and to careful criterion development have been offered as a distinguishing characteristic of work in the field (Blum and Naylor, 1968).

Current interest in performance appraisal issues might thus be considered as nothing more than a continuation of this tradition. However, at least four factors appear to be operating to explain recent fascination with the area. The first is an increased appreciation for the role that performance appraisals play in an integrated system of human resource management in organizations (cf. Cummings and Schwab, 1973). One could always point out that performance appraisal information was central to important decisions relating to employee compensation, demotion, and promotion. It has also long been recognized that such information was essential to the shaping and motivating of specific individuals by using it in feedback sessions with employees. But it is now realized by many that employee appraisals are (or should be) part

Abridged from a chapter in K.M. Rowland and G.D. Ferris, eds., *Research in Personnel and Human Resources Management,* vol. 2, by permission of the publisher, JAI Press Inc., Greenwich, Conn., 1984.

of a system that relates data in this area to employee selection, training, and development, and to career planning and organizational development. Performance appraisal information needs to be fed into these activities and be compatible with them. Moreover, it is becoming increasingly obvious that the way performance appraisal programs are designed and carried out has a profound impact on the reactions employees have to an organization and the rest of its human resources management effort. Therefore it must be considered an important part of this system.

While it is difficult to assert that the publication of a technical paper is a cause or a reflection of a movement in a scientific field, it seems to us that two recent review papers by Landy and Farr (1980) and by DeCotis and Petit (1980), if not initiating interest, at least have invigorated the field. The Landy and Farr paper, in particular, took a needed and critical look at many years of research in the area and pointed out in detail several directions for future work. A fair number of recent papers seem to have been stimulated by this review.

Two other factors appear to have contributed to the increased interest we have noted. Both represent the contexts in which human resource specialists function. The societal and specific organizational milieu of the practitioner in the early 1980s has reflected a tremendous concern for work productivity. Foreign competition and a weakening of national economies worldwide have spurred attention to the determinants (causes) of productivity and a search for ways to improve it. In the spirit of Buckminster Fuller, the goal has been to "do more with less." This has led (reasonably, we think) to an examination of those forces operating on individuals to make them more productive in organizational contexts. Such an examination inevitably highlights the key role of performance appraisals. Productivity will be enhanced, it can be argued, if individuals are directed and motivated properly. A well-designed and implemented appraisal system can do this.

Finally, the intellectual zeitgeist of the human resource specialist has also promoted research on performance appraisal dynamics. In particular, work and theories in many fields of psychology (for instance, social, developmental, human experimental areas) have recently stressed the role of cognition in human affairs. Several lines of research have recently converged to emphasize how we perceive and interpret the behavior of others according to rules of information processing. Many researchers have read and have been stimulated by this work. They have come to see how traditional areas of research can be reinterpreted in exciting ways. Thus, a fair number of recent publications incorporate theories and models of cognitive processing as applied to the making of performance appraisals. And many investigators have entered this area for the first time as a result.

This chapter reviews a great deal of this new work on performance appraisal. It does so by focusing on a set of seven issues or topics. These have been selected by the authors because they meet any one of three criteria. The first criterion is that the area represents one where there seems to be a great deal of research activity as reflected in funded projects, in prepublications, and in publications. The second criterion is that the topic deals with phenomena important to the development of a theory of performance appraisal. That is, in our opinion, the issue examined is critical to the accomplishment of such a goal. The third criterion is based on a recognition that the motive for much of the work on performance appraisal dynamics is to provide guidance to organizational policies and practices. Thus, we have selected some topics because they deal with organizational realities and demands.

In this chapter, the two areas to be considered are (1) person, process, or product measures, and (2) choice of appraisal agent.

A final point to be raised relates to the general structure of each section. Each area will be defined and described. Recent research will be summarized to illustrate what is being done by investigators. Special consideration will be given to directions that we feel are needed in theory building, research, and applications. When appropriate, specific suggestions for research will be made. It is our belief that if work proceeds in the areas we have identified, progress toward understanding and perfecting performance appraisals will occur.

Person, Process, or Product Measures?

Most early performance appraisal systems evaluated managers in terms of the extent to which they possessed the personality characteristics of successful managers. This approach to appraisal reflected prevailing leadership theories during the first half of this century, which focused on personality traits as determinants of successful versus unsuccessful leadership (Stogdill, 1948). Thus, traits such as initiative, dependability, and maturity were prevalent on early forms for appraising both managerial and nonmanagerial personnel.

During the 1950s, researchers (as in the area of leadership) shifted from studying what successful employees *are* to what successful employees *do* and *accomplish*. The difficulties researchers encountered in defining and measuring personality traits led them to focus their attention on studying the observable behaviors of successful individuals (Fleishman, Harris, and Burtt, 1955) and their job-related results (Drucker, 1954). As before, appraisal instruments mirrored this trend with the onset of behavioral checklists and scales (Berkshire and Highland, 1953; Flanagan and Burns, 1955; Smith and Kendall, 1963) and results-oriented approaches (Borgden and Taylor, 1950; Lamouria and Harrell, 1963).

All three types of appraisal content are currently in use by organizations. For instance, a recent survey conducted by the Conference Board regarding managerial appraisal practices revealed that many organizations still use personality traits rather than specific behaviors or results measures on their appraisal forms (Lazar and Wilkstrom, 1977). Out of 61 participating companies, more than half reported employing such factors as initiative, cooperation, judgment, creativity, resourcefulness, innovativeness, and dependability. The viability of the three main content areas is reflected in Campbell, Dunnette, Lawler, and Weick's (1970) *person–product–process* model of managerial effectiveness. The *person* in the model refers to the individual manager's characteristic traits and abilities, *product* to such organizational results as profit maximization and productivity, and *process* to the manager's on-the-job behaviors and activities (Morse and Wagner, 1978). Although Campbell et al. concerned themselves with only managerial effectiveness, the question of whether person, product, and/or process should be appraised applies to all types of organizational jobs. In this section, we will first examine the case for measuring persons, products, and processes, as well as certain combinations. We will then offer our personal views as to what content is best to use.

The Case for Persons, Products, and Processes

The major advocate for appraising traits or "persons" has been Kavanagh (1971). He argues that at present the empirical evidence is not sufficient to accept the "objective traits only" view and to abandon the evaluation of a worker's personality traits. He advocates an open approach for choosing rating stimuli based upon empirical demonstration of validity. He warns against judgmentally discarding rating scale content on a priori grounds and recommends using any trait in the rating form if it helps account for the total variance of the performance appraisal.

Consistent with the "persons" viewpoint is the measurement of managerial effectiveness in terms of what Sokol (1982) terms "managerial competency." This is a characteristic of an individual that leads to behaviors that meet the job demands within the parameters of the organizational environment and that, in turn, bring about desired results. Thus, according to this model, managerial competencies → effective behaviors → effecive performance.

If it is managerial competencies that make the difference between an effective and ineffective manager, then what specifically is a competency? A job competency is an underlying characteristic of a person that results in effective and/or superior performance in a job (Klemp and Spencer, 1980). A competency can consist of a motive, trait, skill, aspect of self-image, social role, or body of knowledge that leads to effective performance (Sokol, 1982). A *motive* is a "recurrent concern for a goal state, or condition, appearing in fantasy, which drives, directs, and selects behavior of the individual" (McClelland, 1971). Examples would include need for achievement and power (McClelland and Winter, 1969) and managerial motivation (Miner, 1978). A *trait* is a set way of responding to a general category of events (for instance, extroversion and behavioral flexibility). A *skill* is the ability to display either a series of related behaviors or mental processes that are functionally related to the completion of a particular task (for instance, logical thinking and attention to detail). An aspect of *self-image* relates to how individuals consciously view themselves. For example, one may see oneself as persuasive and forceful and, as a result, attempt to take the lead in group situations. *Social role* concerns how people define themselves by the role they take on in society. For example, managers who see their roles primarily as professionals will act differently from managers who see their roles as "company men." Finally, a specific *body of knowledge* must be required by the demands of the job in order to qualify as a competency (for instance, knowledge of the product and knowledge of the company–union contract).

One advantage of evaluating individuals in terms of competencies (that is, person variables) according to Sokol (1982) is that they are generic. That is, a single competency is manifest in a number of different actions. For example, the competency of self-control (Boyatizis, 1982) is functioning every time a manager has the urge to do one thing and consciously substitutes another action that results in better performance for the organization. A second advantage of using competencies is that a manager's particular behavior is typically affected by a multitude of competencies. For example, the manager who consistently works overtime is most likely influenced by self-control, need for achievement, and efficiency orientation.

Advocates of using measures of products are quick to point out that both person and process appraisals require some sort of judgment on the part of an evaluator. They contend that there are many kinds of jobs where it is possible to obtain information about performance directly without the necessity of the performance being filtered through the cognitive processes of an appraiser (Cummings and Schwab, 1973). Two main types of products measures can be used: those dealing with production (for example, scrappage, units produced or sold, dollars earned, amount of rejects) and those involving personal (for example, absenteeism, tardiness, injuries, grievances, training time needed to reach some acceptable level of performance) information (Wexley and Yukl, 1977). Sometimes these measures are obtained on individual employees while at times they are aggravated to assess the effectiveness of a particular manager's organizational unit.

Senior-level management, stockholders, and consumers are concerned with economic or cost-related outcomes of their organization (Latham and Wexley, 1977). Thus, advocates of measuring products argue that appraisals should measure managers, as well as their individual subordinates, on the extent to which productivity-based results are satisfactorily achieved (Drucker, 1954; Patton, 1983). The two most common output measuring systems for managers are Management by Objectives (MBO) and Responsibility Centers. MBO involves the joint participation by the manager and the subordinate in the setting of results-oriented goals (outputs which can be measured) rather than focusing on activities to be performed. Under the responsibility-center concept, managers are held responsible for the profits earned by their organizational units, which are designed to be autonomous entities. Managers are credited with the revenue obtained by producing or selling the goods and services of their units to customers and are also charged with all the costs involved in producing such good and services (Carroll and Schneier, 1982). Products measurement is by no means restricted to line manager jobs. It has been successfully used with such diverse jobs as research-managers (Lamouria and Harrell, 1963), multi-line insurance agents (Roach and Wherry, 1970), salespeople (Cravens and Woodruff, 1973), logging truck drivers (Latham and Baldes, 1975), and logging supervisors (Latham and Kinne, 1974).

Advocates of behaviorally-based (that is, process) measures contend that they (1) can account for far more job complexity, (2) can be related more directly to what the employee actually does, (3) are more likely to minimize irrelevant factors not under the employee's control than product measures, (4) can encompass cost-related measures, (5) are far less ambiguous and subjective than person measures, (6) reduce employee role ambiguity by making explicit what behaviors are required of an individual in a given job, and (7) facilitate explicit performance feedback and goal setting in that they encourage meaningful manager–employee discussions regarding the employee's strengths and weaknesses (Latham and Wexley, 1981).

The popularity of behavior-based rating methods was started 21 years ago by Smith and Kendall (1963). They reasoned that different effectiveness levels on job performance rating scales might be anchored using behavioral examples of incumbents' performance (Borman, 1982). Accordingly, they developed what are commonly referred to today as behaviorally anchored rating scales (BARS) or behavioral expectation scales (BES). In recent years, several researchers have experienced difficulties with BARS in field settings and, in response to these difficulties, have suggested alternative systems. The most noteworthy of these newer systems are Behavioral Observation Scales (BOS) (Latham and Wexley, 1981), Behavior Summary Scales (Borman, Hough, and Dunnette, 1976), Behavioral Discrimination Scales (Kane and Lawler, 1979), and Behavioral Assessment Approaches (Komacki, 1981). (A discussion of each of these behaviorally based approaches is beyond the scope of this chapter. The reader is referred to Carroll and Schneler [1982] and Borman [1982] for more information.) Which system is best, if any, must await future empirical research. Although not nearly as popular as MBO and other results-oriented systems, these behavioral approaches are slowly becoming more prevalent as more and more personnel executives conclude that behaviors which are observable, measurable, and job-related should be evaluated (Lazer and Wilkstrom, 1977).

A Proposed Resolution

As we see it, the person–process–product controversy is really a pseudo issue. Each of these types of content has its proper place depending upon the job, the manager's philosophy, and the function of the appraisal information.

Studies have distinguished between control based on direct personal surveillance (behavior control) and control based on the measurement of outputs (output control). Research by Ouchi and Maquire (1975) suggests these two modes of organizational control are independent for the reason that they serve different purposes. Their evidence suggests that output control occurs in response to a manager's need to provide legitimate evidence of performance increases to his or her superior. The less familiar the manager feels her superior is with her performance, the greater her emphasis will be on output control.

Behavioral control seems to be exerted more when the manager's knowledge and the superior's knowledge of the subordinates' jobs increases (Ouchi and Maquire, 1975). Here, the manager and superior understand the means–ends relations (that is, between processes and results) and therefore can provide better developmental feedback. The main factor, however, accounting for the type of control used is the *hierarchical level* of the manager. As managers move up the hierarchy, they rely less on behavioral control since the means–ends relations are less clear at higher levels due to increased job complexity. These findings are consistent with the Conference Board's figures which show that objective setting or MBO increases and behavioral approaches decrease in prevalence as one climbs up the management hierarchy (Lazer and Wilkstrom, 1977).

Another major job characteristic affecting choice of appraisal content is the appraiser's *opportunity to observe*. Obviously, there are certain jobs where neither the manager nor peers see the individual's actions. With the exception perhaps of customers, nobody is available to appraise the individual (for instance, a territorial salesperson) in behavioral terms. In a similar vein, there exist certain jobs that involve covert rather than overt behaviors (for instance, novelist, mathematician, magazine advertisement designer). In these cases, behaviorally based approaches are infeasible.

Results measures are difficult to obtain on employees in many jobs (for example, personnel manager, engineer, chemist). Even when such measures can be obtained, they are affected by numerous situational factors over which the individual employee has little or no control, such as budgetary support, proper maintenance of equipment, availability of raw materials, and sales territory (Peters and O'Connor, 1980; Peters, O'Connor, and Rudolph, 1980). Further, the sole use of these measures can encourage a results-at-all-costs mentality that can run counter to both organizational ethics and productivity. For example, a salesperson might be the best in his company in terms of this year's results, but may be doing this at the expense of his firm's long-term reputation. In these kinds of jobs, results measures are highly suspect since they lack adequate validity.

Certain managers have objected to behaviorally oriented appraisal systems on the grounds that they "stifle creativity," "force me to supervise my people too closely," "remind me of Theory X management," "make me treat my employees like children," and "cause my people to do no more than what's formally expected of them." As one manager told us, "I like to tell my people the results I expect of them, and then let them go out and find their own ways of achieving them. This stretches them. I don't care how they achieve the bottom line, so long as they do." Other managers see this type of thinking as objectionable. They see their managerial role as a coach or helper which means "helping my people to find better ways of performing their jobs," "showing them means to ends," and "reducing their nervousness by letting them know what I expect of them in terms of both results and actions." Obviously, these managers prefer behaviorally oriented systems and differ substantially in their managerial philosophy from the other group.

Performance appraisal information serves many functions within organizations. Four major functions currently served by performance appraisal systems are promotions, development, pay, and layoffs. *Promotion* decisions involve the assessment of an employee's potential. To the extent that the two positions share identical processes and products, behavioral and results-oriented measures can be used. To the extent that the two positions differ, behavioral and results measures on the present job lose their predictive validity and we are forced to use traits which are common across hierarchical positions. For example, one organization appraises its salespeople in terms of getting the job done—the results or what the person has accomplished in meeting the responsibilities of the job. The organization also assesses each salesperson's potential for management by rating the individual on such traits as inner work standards, flexibility, and leadership. It is interesting to point out that Assessment Centers used for promotion purposes tap such "person" dimensions as energy, initiative, creativity, sensitivity, tolerance for stress, and job motivation (Thornton and Byham, 1982).

Results measures by themselves do not tell employees what they need to do to maintain or improve productivity. This does not mean that results measures should be ignored for *development* of employees. Rather, they should be downplayed. They merely communicate to an employee that he is not meeting a set of objectives, but they fail to tell him *why*. For example, telling a production worker that he is not meeting a production standard will not come as any surprise to him since he will already have that information. What he needs to know is what he must *do* differently to improve his productivity. It is for these reasons that behaviorally oriented appraisal systems such as BOS and BARS are essential for employee development (Latham and Wexley, 1981). Developmental feedback in terms of traits causes defensiveness on the part of employees, especially those with low occupational self-esteem (Kay, Meyer, and French, 1966).

We clearly advocate using *pay* to motivate job performance by linking pay increases closely to effective performance and making the relationship as visible to employees as possible (Lawler, 1971). We also contend that employees should be renumerated, where possible, on the basis of *both* their effective behaviors and their results. For example, the authors recently developed an appraisal system for sales managers in a midwestern department store chain. With the current recessed economy, management felt that it was unfair to base pay increases solely on the sales output of each manager's unit. Thus, the chain now uses a combination MBO and BOS appraisal system where results and effective behaviors are each given equal weight. Finally, we contend that *layoffs* should be based on some weighted combination of results, behaviors, and seniority.

Choice of Appraisal Agent

"The ideal rater who observes and evaluates what is important and reports his judgments without bias or appreciable error does not exist, or if he does, we don't know how to separate him from his less effective colleagues (Barrett, 1966, p. 7)." This highlights a dilemma for both researchers and human resource specialists as they attempt to gather performance appraisal information for theory building and testing, and for personnel-related decisions. Research evidence, however, suggests that both personal attributes and role perspectives can have a dramatic effect on the quality of appraisals. Current theory implies that the choice of agent to do the appraisal should depend on the evaluation context as well as the purpose for which the appraisal is being made.

If the issues associated with the choice of individuals in a particular context are complex, the conditions likely to lead to quality appraisals seem well understood (Kane and Lawler, 1978). The person doing the assessment must (1) be in a position to observe the behavior and performance of the individual of interest, (2) be knowledgeable about the dimensions or features of performance, (3) have an understanding of the scale format and the instrument itself, and (4) must be motivated to do a conscientious job of rating. To put it succinctly, the rater should be both willing and able to do the job. Current research, however, suggests that both personal and positional factors affect the extent to which a person can meet these conditions.

Personal Factors

Several investigators have looked at the impact of the personal attributes of the rater on the quality of evaluations made. These qualities emphasized both the ability to understand and evaluate the rating dimensions of interest and the motivation to do so. Several early papers (for example, Mandell, 1956; Schneider and Bayroll, 1953; Kirchner and Reisberg, 1962) stressed such things as job competence of the supervisor. For example, Kirchner and Reisberg (1962) classified raters managers based on how well they themselves were rated on their job performance. The authors found that more effective managers showed more variation in their assessments and were, on the whole, tougher on their subordinates. Kirchner and Reisberg also stressed different factors (for instance, initiative) in their assessments when compared to less effective supervisors (who emphasized cooperation). Similarly, Wagner and Hoover (1974) noted that skilled judges of military drill procedure were less susceptible to a ranking bias in ratings. Finally, on a more theoretical level, Mitchell and Kalb (1981) reported that supervisors with more experience tended to use environmental attributions to describe and interpret the performance of their subordinates.

Related to the skill level of raters are education and experience. Both were found to have an effect on the use of BARS in a police evaluation system (Cascio and Valenzi, 1977). High experience raters tended to give favorable ratings. Supervisors with low levels of education also gave favorable ratings. There was some tendency, however, for higher evaluations to be given to subordinates whose age and experience were similar to the rating officer. Such similarity bias has been well documented in areas other than performance assessment (for instance, Schmitt, 1976).

The search for important rater qualities has also focused on personality. Are there certain types thatt are better able (or willing) to make accurate judgments? An early review article by Taft (1955) concludes that there is evidence for a positive answer to this question. This position has found additional support in more recent work by Borman (1979). By presenting examples of performance to be rated on videotape, Borman was able to compute an accuracy index for each of his subjects. He then related this index to scores on a large variety of personality and biographical inventories which were also administered to subjects. Borman found that 17 percent of the variance in the differential accuracy of ratings was accounted for by these measures. A profile of the more accurate perceiver suggests that the personal qualities related to accuracy include verbal reasoning, freedom from self-doubt, high self-control, and a detail orientation. He also notes that these qualities are similar to those identified in the literature dealing with the correlates of accuracy in person perception in general. Borman speculates that certain individual differences may be related to accuracy across a wide range of situations or tasks (for instance, interviews, performance appraisals) while others are more specific.

One specific attribute that has attracted a great deal of interest relates to the rater's information processing capacity. For example, field independence was examined by Gruenfeld and Arbuthnot (1969) using such measures as the rod and frame test and the embedded figures test. The former was found to correlate with several indices of variability in ratings made by a sample of nurses. Because of this, the authors concluded that those who are relatively field independent would make better raters.

More work has been done indexing information processing using measures of cognitive complexity. Schneier (1977) introduced the notion that a rater's cognitive complexity, measured by a modified version of the Bieri Role Repertory Grid Measure, would affect preferences for the type of rating scale to be used. More specifically, high complexity subjects were thought to perform better (rate more accurately) on more complex scales, such as BARS. In his study, such individuals were more confident with the BARS format, preferred it in use, and exhibited ratings with less leniency and greater variation in the scores given.

While Schneier's proposition is appealing, recent research (Borman, 1979; Bernardin, Cardy and Carlile, 1982; Lahey and Saal, 1981; Sanser and Pond, 1981) has not been able to support it. For example, the high complexity subjects in Bernardin et al. did not demonstrate superior quality ratings on BARS nor did they prefer the more complex scale format. Lahey and Saal found no differences in leniency or range restriction, either as a function of rater's cognitive complexity or as a complexity by scale format interaction. Rater confidence was also uncorrelated to the variables of interest. While individual differences may be related to rating quality and scale preference, cognitive complexity does not seem to be one of them.

Organization Role or Position

In most organizations the person doing the performance appraisal is the supervisor. This can be considered reasonable since the supervisor is frequently able to observe the behavior and performance of employees and certainly should be knowledgeable about the factors defining effectiveness. But in most organizations there are other agents in a position to provide evaluations. Barrett (1966) identifies other potential sources of appraisal information as the employee himself, others at the same level as the employee (peers), the employee's own subordinates and personnel specialists. He concludes that for certain purposes, these less frequently used raters appear to offer great benefits to an appraisal program. However, accumulating evidence suggests that the role or position of the rater has a great impact on the nature of the assessments made. Data from differing positions should not be considered interchangeable.

On a general level, supervisors and subordinates frequently disagree on what constitutes the basis for effective performance. O'Reilly (1973) found that raters at different organizational levels have different ideas about what tasks are most important to the job. This became clear to Zedeck and his associates (Zedeck et al., 1974) as they tried to develop behaviorally anchored ratings scales. Managers at different organizational levels used different critical behavior examples in their definition of good and poor job performance.

The actual ratings made by those in differing organizational roles or positions have been compared and contrasted in a number of studies. Heneman (1974) related self-ratings of employees to those of their supervisor on nine scales. He found some evidence of convergence but little discriminant validity. Similarly, Klimoski and London (1974) obtained ratings from hospital nurses, their supervisors, and their peers. A hierarchical factor analysis of the combined sets of ratings confirmed the existence of a bias related to the perspective of the raters. Raters in different positions used different dimensions in assessment. This was defined as a "justifiable halo" reflecting differences in such things as value, expectations, and opportunities to observe the work being done. Moreover, these findings were replicated by Holzbach (1978) in his study of managers and professionals. Dimensionality differed by the source of ratings. He obtained evidence of a strong rater group-specific halo. In this study supervisors' ratings seemed to be influenced by job specific factors and were related to overall effectiveness assessments. In contrast, peer and self-ratings did not appear to differentiate among job behaviors. Thus, if multiple criterion measures are desired, supervisors ratings would be most useful.

The issues of the relationship (comparability) of ratings from different roles of sources is intimately tied up with the use of multi-trait multi-method matrix analysis (MTMM) in criterion development (for instance, Kavanagh et al., 1971). The MTMM approach is often used to establish the construct validity of criterion measures. If, however, the multiple methods used are raters from these different roles or positions (as in Klimoski and London, 1974), for this analysis to work one must assume that they are able to provide comparable evaluations. The studies reported above calls this into question. It may not be reasonable to expect the ratings to converge, and thus the pattern of intercorrelations in MTMM analysis must be reinterpreted in this light.

Borman (1974) feels that it is unrealistic to demand such convergence. He argues that people at different levels observe significantly different facets of a ratee's job. If you are to expect convergence it should only be after controlling for such things as organizational level. In his study, he found distinctively different dimensions of effectiveness for a secretary's job (who supervise secretaries) and for other secretaries (peers). On the other hand, there was a reasonable amount of within-level inter-rater agreement. Borman goes on to suggest (in the absence of evidence to the contrary) that the different perspectives should be considered equally valid. So one might conceivably want both points of view. He does stress that if this were to be done one should only get ratings on dimensions appropriate to that rater group's perspective. If, however, conditions are likely to encourage a similar perspective across sources (for example, all levels have an equal knowledge of the job in question, all know the incumbents and can observe their work) one might expect convergent validity. Then the same dimensions might be tapped by all groups of raters. This is what appears to have occurred in a study reported by Albrecht et al. (1964). Still, a definitive test of these notions has yet to be performed.

Dealing with Organizational Realities

The studies reviewed suggest that individuals differ in their ability to make quality ratings and that individuals in particular organizational roles or positions differ on this as well. In this regard, it seems difficult to generalize with regard to who should provide operational ratings. Kane and Lawler (1978) suggest that multiple sources of performance appraisal information would be desirable. However they warn that the appropriateness of using peers or self-ratings, for example, would depend on the other parts of the appraisal system. The traits, behaviors, or outcomes assessed by a particular perspective depend on such things as technology, reward structure, and task interdependency. In general, they concur with Borman (1974) that each perspective holds a piece of the puzzle of the picture of an employee's past and present performance. In the end they recommend that several levels or roles should contribute to assessment but only based upon those performance dimensions particularly appropriate for them to assess. Even then we must still be concerned with potential differences among rater groups in motivation to evaluate accuracy (see Schneier and Beatty, 1978).

If specific individuals or groups of individuals are known to differ in their ability to assess various components of effectiveness, perhaps their multiple perspectives might be combined in the manner of a composite criterion. This would acknowledge the potential for increased validity due to the more complete coverage of a true or ultimate criterion which is (by definition) complex. Performance assessment data from diffferent sources might be weighted and combined statistically to provide such a composite (Guion, 1965, p. 473).

A particular feature of organizational reality that would appear to affect the quality of the data obtained from different sources is the purpose of the appraisal. It seems clear that the motivation to evaluate accurately (and hence the quality of the ratings made) would be strongly influenced by whether the ratings are being made for research, for administrative reasons, or for employee development. For example, self-ratings are notoriously inflated if they are perceived to be used for some administrative decision (DeNisi and Shaw, 1977; Thornton, 1980). Yet in the context of self-analysis for self-development they can be very good at indexing a person's strengths and weaknesses (Mabe and West, 1982). Even in selection settings (where strategic self-presentation is expected) conditions can be created to promote candid or accurate self-assessments (Primoff, 1980). Similarly, peer ratings can be thought of as potentially the most accurate judgments of employee behavior (Barrett, 1966; Shranger and Osberg, 1981) or viewed as fraught with numerous problems (DeNisi and Mitchell, 1978). Both images are correct but dependent on the purpose to which the ratings are placed. As a generalization, we would predict the highest levels of motivation to be accurate across these various sources under conditions aimed at employee development and renewal.

One last example of the impact of the reality of organizational life on the choice of rater is worth highlighting. This is the nature and quality of the relationships among rater and ratees. As mentioned in the previous section, most work has been done examining the dynamics between supervisors and their subordinates. Based on these and other papers, it seems clear that the selection of individuals or groups for purposes of providing assessment information should consider the interpersonal dynamics of the appraisal setting as well (see also Kipnis et al., 1980; Grey and Kipnis, 1976).

References

Albrecht, P.A., Glaser, E.M., and Marks, J. Validation of a multiple assessment procedure for managerial personnel. *Journal of Applied Psychology,* 1964, *48,* 351–360.

Barrett, R.S. *Performance Rating.* Chicago, Illinois: Science Research Associates, 1966.

Bernardin, H.J., Cardy, R.L., and Carlyle, J.J. Cognitive complexity and appraisal effectiveness: Back to the drawing board? *Journal of Applied Psychology,* 1982, *67,* 151–160.

Blum, M.L., and Naylor, J.C. *Industrial psychology: Its theoretical and social foundations.* New York: Harper & Row, 1968.

Borman, W.C. The rating of individuals in organizations: An alternate approach. *Organizational Behavior and Human Performance,* 1974, *12,* 105–124.

————. Individual differences correlates of accuracy in evaluating others' performance effectiveness. *Applied Psychological Measurement,* 1979, *3,* 103–115.

————. Behavioral approaches to evaluating individuals' work performance. Paper presented at John Hopkins University Conference on Performance Assessment. Washington, D.C., November, 1982.

Borman, W.C., Hough, L.M., and Dunnette, M.D. *Development of behaviorally based ratings scales for evaluating the performance of U.S. Navy recruiters.* Navy Personnel Research and Development Center Technical Report TR-76-31, 1976.

Boyatzis, R.E. *The competent manager: A model for effective performance.* New York: Wiley, 1982.

Campbell, J.P., Dunnette, M.D., Lawler, E.E., III, and Weick, K.E. *Managerial behavior, performance and effectiveness.* New York: McGraw-Hill, 1970.

Carroll, S.J., and Schneier, C.E. *Performance appraisal and review systems.* Glenview, Ill.: Scott, Foresman, 1982.

Cascio, W.F., and Valenzi, E.R. Behaviorally anchored rating scales: Effects of education and job experience of raters and ratees. *Journal of Applied Psychology,* 1977, *62,* 278–282.

Cravens, D.W., and Woodruff, R.B. An approach for determining criteria of sales performance. *Journal of Applied Psychology,* 1973, *57,* 242–247.

Cummings, L.L., and Schwab, D.P. *Performance in organizations: Determinants and appraisal.* Glenview, Illinois: Scott, Foreman, 1973.

DeCotiis, T., and Petit, A. The performance appraisal process: A model and some testable propositions. *Academy of Management Review,* 1978, *3,* 635–646.

DeNisi, A., and Mitchell, J. An analysis of peer ratings as predictors and criterion measures. *Academy of Management Review,* 1978, *3,* 369–373.

DeNisi, A.S., Shaw, J.B. Investigation of the uses of self-reports of abilities. *Journal of Applied Psychology,* 1977, *62,* 641–644.

Drucker, P.F. *The practice of management.* New York: Harper and Row, 1954.

Flanagan, J.C., and Burns, R.K. The employee performance record: A new appraisal and development tool. *Harvard Business Review,* 1955, *33,* 95–102.

Fleishman, E.A., Harris, E.F., and Burtt, H.E. *Leadership and supervision in industry.* Columbus: Bureau of Educational Research, Ohio State University, 1955.

Grey, R.J., and Kipnis, D. Untangling the performance appraisal dilemma: The influence of perceived organizational context on evaluative processes. *Journal of Applied Psychology,* 1976, *61,* 329–335.

Gruenfeld, L., and Arbuthnot, J. Field independence as a conceptual framework for prediction of variability in ratings of others. *Perceptual and Motor Skills,* 1969, *28,* 31–44.

Guion, R.M. *Personnel testing.* New York: McGraw-Hill, 1965.

Heneman, H.G. Comparisons of self- and superior-rating of managerial performance. *Journal of Applied Psychology,* 1974, *59,* 638–642.

Holzbach, R.L. Rater bias in performance ratings: Superior, self-, and peer ratings. *Journal of Applied Psychology,* 1978, *63,* 579–588.

Kane, J.S., and Lawler, E.E., III. Methods of peer assessment. *Psychological Bulletin,* 1978, *85,* 555–586.

Kane, J.S., and Lawler, E.E. Performance appraisal effectiveness: Its assessment and determinants. *Research in Organizational Behavior,* 1979, *1,* 425–478.

Kavanagh, M.J. The content issue in performance appraisal: A review. *Personnel Psychology,* 1971, *24,* 653–668.

Kavanagh, M., MacKinney, A.C., and Wolens, L. Issues in managerial performance: Multi-trait–multi-method analysis of rating. *Psychological Bulletin,* 1971, *75(1),* 34.

Kipnis, D., Schmidt, S., Price, K., and Stitt, C. Why do I like thee: Is it your performance or my orders? *Journal of Applied Psychology,* 1980, *66,* 324–328.

Kirchner, W.K., and Reisberg, D.J. Differences between better and less-effective supervisors in appraisal of subordinates. *Personnel Psychology,* 1962, *15,* 295–302.

Klemp, G.O., Jr., and Spencer, L.M., Jr. *Job competence assessment.* Boston: McBer and Company, 1980.

Klimoski, R.J., and London, M. Role of the rater in performance appraisal. *Journal of Applied Psychology,* 1974, *59,* 445–451.

Komacki, J. Behavioral measurements: Toward solving the criterion problem. Paper presented at the American Psychological Association Convention, Los Angeles, August 1981.

Lahey, M.A., and Saal, F.E. Evidence incompatible with a cognitive compatibility theory of rating behavior. *Journal of Applied Psychology,* 1981, *66,* 706–715.

Lemouria, L.H., and Harrell, T.W. An approach to an objective criterion for research managers. *Journal of Applied Psychology,* 1963, *47,* 353–357.

Landy, F.J., and Farr, J.L. Performance rating. *Psychological Bulletin,* 1980, *87,* 72–107.

Latham, G.P., and Baldes, J.J. The "practical significance" of Locke's theory of goal setting. *Journal of Applied Psychology,* 1975, *60,* 122–124.

Latham, G.P., and Kinne, S.B. Improving job performance through training in goal setting. *Journal of Applied Psychology,* 1974, *59,* 187–191.

Latham, G.P., and Wexley, K.N. *Increasing productivity through performance appraisal.* Reading, Massachusetts: Addison–Wesley, 1981.

Lawler, E.E. *Pay and organizational effectiveness: A psychological view.* New York: McGraw–Hill, 1971.

Lazer, R.I., and Wilkstrom, W.S. *Appraising managerial performance: Current practices and future direction.* New York: The Conference Board, 1977.

Mabe, P.A., III, and West, S.G. Validity of self-evaluation of ability: A review and meta-analysis. *Journal of Applied Psychology,* 1982, *67,* 280–296.

McClelland, D.C. *Assessing human motivation.* New York: General Learning Press, 1971.

McClelland, D.C., and Winter, D.G. *Motivating economic achievement.* New York: Free Press, 1969.

Mandell, M.M. Supervisory characteristics and ratings. *Personnel,* 1956, *32,* 435–440.

Miner, J.B. Twenty years of research on role motivation theory of managerial effectiveness. *Personnel Psychology,* 1978, *31,* 739–760.

Mitchell, T.R., and Kalb, L.S. Effects of outcome knowledge and outcome valence on supervisors' evaluations. *Journal of Applied Psychology,* 1981, *66,* 604–612.

Morse, J.J., and Wagner, F.R. Measuring the process of managerial effectiveness. *Academy of Management Journal,* 1978, *21,* 23–35.

O'Reilly, A.P. Skill requirements: Supervisor–subordinate conflict. *Personnel Psychology,* 1973, *26,* 75–80.

Ouchi, W.G., and Maguire, M.A. Organizational control: Two functions. *Administrative Science Quarterly,* 1975, *20,* 559–569.

Patton, T.H., Jr. *A manager's guide to performance appraisal.* New York: Free Press, 1982.

Peters, L.H., and O'Connor, E.J. Situational constraints and work outcomes: The influence of a frequently overlooked construct. *Academy of Management Review,* 1980, *5,* 391–397.

Peters, L.H., O'Connor, E.J., and Rudolf, C.J. The behavioral and effective consequences of performance-relevant situational variables. *Organizational Behavior and Human Performance*, 1980, *25*, 79–86.

Primoff, E.S. The use of self-assessments in examining. *Personnel Psychology*, 1980, *33*, 283–290.

Roach, D.E., and Wherry, R.J., Sr. Performance dimensions of multi-line insurance agents. *Personnel Psychology*, 1970, *23*, 239–250.

Schmitt, N. Social and situational determinants of interview decisions: Implications for the employment interview. *Personnel Psychology*, 1976, *29*, 79–101.

Schneider, D.E., and Bayroll, A.G. The relationship between rater characteristics and the validity of ratings. *Journal of Applied Psychology*, 1953, *31*, 278–280.

Schneier, C.E. Operational utility and psychometric characteristics of behavioral expectation scales: A cognitive reinterpretation. *Journal of Applied Psychology*, 1977, *62*, 541–548.

Schneier, C.G., and Beatty, R.W. The influence of role prescriptions on the performance appraisal process. *Academy of Management Journal*, 1978, *21*, 129–135.

Shrauger, J.S., and Osberg, T.M. The relative accuracy of self-predictions and judgments by others in psychological assessment. *Psychological Bulletin*, 1981, *90*, 322–351.

Smith, P., and Kendall, L.M. Retranslation of expectations: An approach to the construction of unambiguous anchors for rating scales. *Journal of Applied Psychology*, 1963, *47*, 149–155.

Sokol, M. Managerial competency. Paper presented at The Johns Hopkins University Conference on Performance Assessment. Washington, D.C., November, 1982.

Stogdill, R.M. Personal factors associated with leadership: A survey of the literature. *Journal of Psychology*, 1948, *25*, 35–71.

Taft, R. The ability to judge people. *Psychological Bulletin*, 1955, *52*, 1–23.

Thornton, G. Psychometric properties of self-appraisal of job performance. *Personnel Psychology*, 1980, *33*, 263–271.

Wagner, E.E., and Hoover, T.O. The influence of technical knowledge on position error in ranking. *Journal of Applied Psychology*, 1974, *59*, 406–407.

5 Stress in Organizations: Human Resource Challenge and Opportunity

Randall S. Schuler

Importance of Stress in Organizations

There are four major reasons why stress in organizations is becoming such a prominent topic of discussion and research by individuals working in organizations as well as by those studying individuals in organizations.

Health

The World Health Organization defines *health* as the presence of physical and psychological well-being. With this definition of health, a review of the research on stress plainly indicates that stress may be "hazardous to one's health." Some of the major ill-health indicators associated with stress in organizations are neuroses, coronary heart disease (CHD), alimentary conditions such as dyspepsia and ulcers, cancer, asthma, high blood pressure, backache, and the related use of alcohol and drugs. In addition to the increased susceptibility of these ill-health indicators to those working in stressful conditions, there is the increased likelihood of incurring accidents on the job when under stress.

Financial Impact

It is estimated that the economic cost of peptic ulcers and cardiovascular disease alone in the United States is about $45 billion annually. The cost to society and organizations of the stress-related symptom of backache is also high. Based on a survey conducted by the National Centers for Health Statistics in 1977, backache was the fifth most common reason for visits to office-based physicians in 1975. In 1976, 14.2 percent of the disability claims filed by companies for individuals and 17.7 percent of the benefits paid involved back disorder. Table 5–1

Table 5–1
Costs of Stress of Executives

	Conservative Estimate	Ultraconservative Estimate
Cost of executive work loss days (salary)	$2,861,775,800	$1,430,887,850
Cost of executive hospitalization	248,316,864	124,158,432
Cost of executive outpatient care	131,058,235 ·	65,529,117
Cost of executive mortality	16,470,977,439	8,235,488,720
	$19,712,128,238	$9,856,064,119

Adapted from Greenwood (1978).

shows estimated costs of stress that executives undergo. Although these figures are only estimates of the financial impact, they do offer reasons for the concern over stress in organizations. Nonetheless, these data do not necessarily provide a convincing case for immediate action by organizations to reduce or even manage employee stress. Furthermore, employee stress may not be a result of organizational conditions, but rather of conditions outside the work place.

This being the case, should organizations do anything more than regard the effects of stress as merely a part of doing business? It appears that many organizations have already answered this question affirmatively, with the development and implementation of strategies to deal with stress in organizations. Their resolution to confront the issue of stress in organizations is based in part on the view that stress is a financial threat and a threat to the effectiveness of the entire organization.

Organizational Effectiveness

The increasing concern shown by some organizations about stress reflects an expanded definition of it and a basis on which to evaluate organizational effectiveness or success. Although many organizations still utilize profit or productivity as the main basis on which to evaluate how well the organization is doing, other organizations and observers of organizations are recognizing the need for several bases on which to evaluate organizations. This need is evident from viewing organizations as open systems rather than as closed, self-sufficient systems. Consistent with this description of organizations as open systems are the assumptions that (1) some means have to be devoted to such non-goal functions as service and custodial activities, including means employed for the maintenance of the organization itself, and (2) the employees and society have as much of a stake in what the organization is and does as the organization and its managers.

Thus, with an open systems view of organizations it is necessary and legitimate to evaluate organizations on the basis of employee satisfaction, health, accidents, turnover, and absenteeism, as well as in efficiency, profitability, productivity, and return on investment. And since stress in organizations is related to many of these bases, stress itself becomes a necessary and legitimate concern for organizations.

Legal Compliance and Worker Compensation

Worker compensation laws now make an employer legally liable for an employee's mental illness as well as physical illness, whatever its cause, if is aggravated, accelerated, precipitated, or triggered to the point of disability or need for medical care by any condition of the employment. Furthermore, fault or absence of fault on the part of the employee or employer has no bearing on the determination of liability of the employer for payment of worker compensation benefits. Thus, it is only sufficient for an employee to show that an illness was precipitated by an organization even to claim compensation, regardless of other non-organizational events to which the individual may have been exposed. This suggests then that organizations should become concerned with the effects of stress regardless of whether the individual comes to work already stressed or not.

Organizations also need to be concerned with stress because they are legally responsible for the presence of stressful conditions according to the Occupational Safety and Health Act (OSHA) of 1970. According to the act, the employer is liable for both physical conditions causing an employee physical harm (for instance, chemical poisons and physical obstructions) and sociopsychological conditions causing an employee mental or psychological harm (OSHA regulations, 1970). Although the impact of OSHA may have been somewhat diminished by the ruling forbidding unannounced entry to organizations, it is still a potent force and one whose influence is likely to increase. The research arm of OSHA, the National Institute of Occupational Safety and Health, (NIOSH) has been and is funding extensive research programs regarding stress in organizations.

NIOSH's primary goals are to identify conditions associated with stress or at least the symptoms of stress and develop strategies by which to deal with stress. But crucial to the attainment of these goals is an understanding of what stress is.

What is Stress?

Stress is defined here as a *perceived dynamic state involving uncertainty about something important.* The dynamic state can be associated with opportunities or constraints. States of opportunity are perceived by the individual to offer the potential fulfillment of important needs and values. States of constraint are perceived to be blocking or preventing current fulfillment of important needs and values.

Stress can be associated with positive (an opportunity) or negative (a constraint) events. For example, a promotion can be perceived as a positive stress if the employee thinks that the promotion will lead to valued outcomes but is uncertain about whether he or she can succeed or not in the new job. An example of negative stress is where an individual perceives that he or she has a job that is meaningless and really wants to get out of the situation (because it does not satisfy any important values) but is not sure how.

Sources of Stress

Common stressors (positive as well as negative) experienced by people include

The pressure of time and deadlines

Experiencing rapid and multiple changes

Never having enough time to accomplish everything

Fear of failure

Being unsure about career and life directions

Working in a role whose responsibilities are unclear or viewed differently by different people in authority

Disliking a job or finding it unfulfilling but not knowing what to do about it

Lack of communication

Lack of social support and positive acceptance

Pressure for immediate results

Lack of control

Interpersonal conflicts

Pay inequities

Poor supervision

Task uncertainty

Effects of Stress

The effects of stress on individuals can be grouped into three categories: physiological, psychological and behavioral. Included in each
category are several effects. The physiological effects include, in the
short term, increased heartrate, increased respirations, and headaches,
and in the long term, ulcers, increased blood pressure, and heart attacks. The psychological effects include

Apathy, resignation, boredom

Regression

Fixation

Projection

Negativism

Fantasy

Forgetfulness

Tendency to misjudge people

Uncertainty about whom to trust

Inability to organize self

Inner confusion about duties or roles

Dissatisfaction

High intolerance for ambiguity and not dealing well with new or
strange situations

Tunnel vision

Tendency to begin vacillating in decision making

Tendency to become distraught with trifles

Inattentiveness: loss of power to concentrate

Loss of responsibility

Loss of concern for the organization

Irritability

Procrastination

Feelings of persecution

Gut-level feelings of unexplainable dissatisfaction

The behavioral effects can be subdivided into individual and organizational effects. The *individual* consequences of stress include

Loss of appetite

Sudden, noticeable loss or gain of weight

Sudden change of appearance: decline or improvement in dress; sudden change of complexion (sallow, reddened, acne), sudden change of hair style or length

Difficult breathing

Sudden change of smoking habits

Sudden change in use of alcohol

The *organizational* consequences of stress include

Low performance in quality or quantity

Absenteeism

Voluntary turnover

Accident proneness

Since many of these effects of stress are undesirable, individuals and organizations are inclined to eliminate or reduce stress. Often preventing them from acting to reduce or eliminate stress, however, is indecision over what to do. Here are some brief suggestions as to what individuals and organizations can do to cope with stress.

Individual Strategies to Cope with Stress

Occasionally, people are their own worst enemies, creating stress by their actions, behaviors, and attitudes. In these cases, they must develop strategies to use on themselves rather than on others.

Stress management strategies enable people to cut their losses and to take advantage of a situation. The fourteen strategies offered here can help any individual cope more constructively with stressful situations.

1. Perceive situations as challenges rather than problems. Taking this attitude makes it easier to play down the adverse effects of situations and accentuate the positive. People who perceive situations this way often have certain other attitudes toward life: openness to change, a feeling of involvement in their activities, and a sense of control over their lives.

2. Behave more like a Type B than a Type A person. Friedman and Rosenman suggest that Type A people are more likely to suffer from coronary heart disease than are Type B's. Consequently, it may be worthwhile to consider switching from Type A to Type B. Type A people tend to move, walk, and eat rapidly; explosively accentuate words in ordinary speech, whether necessary or not, and rapidly utter the last few words of sentences; strive to think or do several things at once; find it difficult to refrain from raising subjects of personal interest in conversation; feel vaguely guilty when they relax; and experience a chronic sense of time urgency, of constant struggle, which Rosenman and Friedman identify as the "kernel" of Type A behavior. Type B people tend to be free of the habits and traits that characterize the Type A person; lack a sense of time urgency; seldom harbor free-floating hostility or feel the need to display their achievements; play for play's sake, finding fun and relaxation rather than competition; and relax without guilt.

3. Consider changing parts of your life or job that engender chronic stress. Discuss the situation with a friend, someone in authority, or employees. Many will appreciate your raising a problem from which they suffer also. Perhaps your supervisor has given you too many responsibilities or has not communicated clearly. Either condition causes uncertainty and stress. To apply this principle, however, requires acting on the next one simultaneously.

4. Be open and positively assertive. Convince yourself that you are worthwhile and important as anyone else. Remember that unless you are assertive, people will not recognize a stressful situation. To talk openly with others, especially with those in authority, is difficult. People with self-esteem are able to confront others this way. Do not avoid the confrontation, force a solution, or minimize the importance of your stress.

5. Use some time management techniques. People often cause themselves stress by taking on too much at once or performing unrewarding tasks. They are unwilling to change the situation because they

do not know what they really want. A key strategy is to become aware of your job duties, authority, and responsibility, and their importance; your skills, needs, and abilities; and how your time is allocated on the job. A suggested technique for sharpening this awareness is to keep a daily or weekly activity log with a detailed analysis of what, who, where, and how much time each activity requires.

Once a high level of awareness is achieved, the next three steps of time management are conserving time, controlling time, and creating time.

Conserving time includes using form letters, curtailing meetings, and speed reading. Controlling time means scheduling activities more realistically, budgeting time, and avoiding procrastination. Creating time includes more effective planning, being more decisive, and clarifying roles and policies.

6. Analyze your roles. Who expects what of you? Can you meet the expectations? Do you want to meet them? What expectations do you have of others? Are they realistic? Determine whether your roles match your needs and values, and manage your roles.

Role analysis is closely related to the first five principles. Before changing parts of your life or job, know what they are and why you want to change. If you change jobs, will there by new roles to perform? Learn about these roles, decide whether you want them, and plan for the change. Similarly, leaving a job requires abandoning roles.

7. Plan a response to stress. Plan how to react to a termination, a raise, an interview, or any peak moment. Delay an event if necessary to prepare adequately. Get plenty of rest before the big event.

8. Take stock of your own power and the situation you face. Work with the idea that you have the power to control your response to stress.

9. Take it easy. Nothing is gained by worry. Do what you can about a situation, affirming that you have done your best and that everything will work out well.

10. Experiment with ways to calm yourself. Engage in yoga or meditation or find a quiet place free of disturbances. Take a walk.

11. Do something you enjoy to manage stress. If you don't like to walk, try a massage or a hot bath. Go to a baseball game or a movie.

12. Design a calm environment for quieting. Change the environment within which you work. Hold telephone calls or work while everyone else is at lunch.

13. Nurture some inner peace. Allow yourself to feel purposeful, valuable, and respected by society. Try to find ways of expression that are so involving you can lose yourself in them, yet find yourself.

14. Engage in a good diet and regular exercise.

**Organizational Strategies to Help Individuals Cope
with Stress**

There are numerous ways by which stress in organizations can be dealt
with by organizations. It should be noted parenthetically that the concern for stress in organizations and strategies to deal with it are not
and should not be limited to the organizations themselves or the individuals within them. For example, in the United States, OSHA,
NOISH and the Center for Occupational Mental Health (COMH) at
Cornell represent two federal and one private organization also concerned with stress in organizations. Furthemore, concern for stress in
organizations is not limited to the United States. In fact, in many other
nations the concern for stress is legislated to a much greater degree
than in the United States. In the Scandinavian countries, for example,
employers are required, in some instances, to provide meaningful work
and appropriate job satisfaction with a minimum of occupational stress.
In addition there are two world associations, the International Com-
mittee on Occupational Mental Health (ICOMH) and the permanent
Commission and International Association on Occupational Health,
designed to promote interdisciplinary communication and understanding of stress.

Specific programs that organizations may implement should be
based on the specific needs of the organization. Often these can be
identified by means of questionnaires and interviews conducted by the
human resource department.

At TRW (due in part to employee demand, general dissatisfaction,
and new policies and procedures due to Federal and State legislation),
several steps to stress management and reduction were implemented,
including (1) Crisis-counseling training sessions with the industrial relations staff; (2) increasing the employees' general awareness of stress
and what they can do about it; (3) adding stress discussions to the
supervisory training program; (4) adding a module on stress to the
middle management programs; and (5) offering after-hours programs
such as workshops in the use of biofeedback, meditation exercises, and
other relaxation techniques. Also based on the nature of the situation
(for instance, reorganizations) Pennsylvania Bell held special seminars
where executives could discuss their life changes (since such changes
often cause personal and job problems), identify their own strengths
and weaknesses in adapting to the changes, and then develop methods
to adopt. "So far, it seems to be working," one manager commented.
Before the seminar, it was a policy not to bring personal problems to
the job; now, "the word's out, so to speak—it's O.K. to feel frustrated,
it's O.K. to feel stress".

Organizations can also reduce stress by making sure employees know what is expected of them, know what is rewarded and punished, and know how to perform their jobs. Organizations can enhance employees' jobs, giving them a greater sense of self-control. It appears at this time that employees are much better off when they are able to experience control. Organizations can also create supportive work environments, offer job security, and train supervisors. Fortunately, organizations are recognizing the importance of stress and are taking action to deal with it.

Now with this greater willingness on the part of some organizations and individuals to be more open about and deal with stress, and based upon the understanding of stress we have presented here, the major questions remaining are: What *will* researchers and organizations be doing about stress in organizations in the future; and what *should* researchers and organizations be doing about stress in organizations in the future? It is anticipated that these two questions and others will be addressed in our conference.

Summary

Stress and its effects are important to individuals and organizations. Fortunately, stress and its effects can be managed. Individuals can act alone to cope with their stress, and organizations can implement strategies to help individuals cope. How individuals should cope and what organizations should do are not always easy to determine. This, however, is where the organization's human resource manager can play a critical role. The manager can offer programs and advice for individuals to cope and can diagnose organizational conditions to determine appropriate organizational strategies. Although playing this role is a challenge, it provides tremendous opportunity for the organization and its employees as well as for the human resource manager.

6

An Integrative Transactional Process Model of Stress in Organizations

Randall S. Schuler

Introduction

Stress in organizations is a rapidly growing concern to organizational researchers and management practitioners because of its relationships with a magnitude of costly individual and organizational symptoms. (Schuler, 1980; McLean, 1979; Greenwood, 1978). Associated with this rapid growth is the tendency for many, and in some cases almost all, traditional organizational phenomena to be labelled as stressors or stressful. In addition, traditional organizational outcomes, such as satisfaction and performance, are being viewed as symptoms of stress. Nevertheless, not all aspects of organizations are stressors, although they have the potential to be so, nor are satisfaction and performance the only stress symptoms which should be of concern to researchers and practitioners.

Because stress can be so costly, academics and practitioners should focus their efforts on dealing with stress, for instance by affecting potential stressors in organizations and developing strategies by which individuals can most effectively manage or reduce their stress. This change, however, is not an easy one, particularly when almost every aspect of an organization is labelled as stressful or a stressor. Fortunately, the task can be facilitated by offering a precise definition of stress in organizations. The definition presented here is critical because it will aid in specifying which and how aspects of an organization are really stressors. Furthermore, this definition will serve as a base upon which to construct a model of stress to integrate these aspects of an organization with individual characteristics.

Thus the purposes of this chapter are to: (1) offer a definition of

Reprinted from the *Journal of Occupational Behaviour*, vol. 3 (1982): 5–19. Copyright © 1982 by John Wiley & Sons, Ltd. Reprinted by permission of John Wiley & Sons, Ltd.

Portions of this paper are taken from Schuler, R.W., Definition and conceptualization of stress in organizations, *Organizational Behavior and Human Performance*, April 1980, 184–215.

stress; (2) present an integrative transactional process model of stress which integrates previous research and literature on stress; (3) suggest how individuals can deal with stress; and (4) propose several testable research hypotheses based on the definition and model of stress presented. In presenting the definition and model of stress, past research and literature will be drawn upon where appropriate. They will be used, however, only within the context of the definition and model presented. More thorough reviews and criticisms can be found of these in several excellent sources (see McLean, 1979; Cooper and Marshall, 1976; Cox, 1978; Schuler, 1980; Cooper and Payne, 1978, 1979; Beehr and Newman, 1978).[1]

What Is Stress in Organizations?

Stress has been defined in numerous ways. A review of four of these definitions will provide the basis for the definition of stress to be used here. Selye (1956) defined *stress as the non-specific response to any demand*. Stress, according to French, Rogers and Cobb (1974) *is a misfit between a person's skills and abilities and demands of the job, and a misfit in terms of a person's needs supplied by the environment.* Beehr and Newman (1978) define (job) *stress as a condition wherein job-related factors interact with the worker to change (disrupt or enhance) his/her psychological or physiological condition such that the person (mind and/or body) is forced to deviate from normal functioning.* And lastly McGrath (1976) defines stress in terms of a set of conditions having stress in it: "Stress involves an interaction of person and environment. Something happens 'out there' which presents a person with a demand, or a constraint or an opportunity for behaviour."

Based upon these definitions and others not reviewed here (for example, see Cox, 1978 and McLean, 1979), stress is defined here as *a perceived dynamic state involving uncertainty about something important.* The dynamic state can be associated with opportunities, constraints or demands (note: these terms were also used by McGrath, 1976 but are extended here in more detail). States of opportunity are perceived by the individual to offer the potential fulfillment of important needs and values. States of constraint are perceived to be blocking or preventing current fulfillment of important needs and values. States of demand are those of the physical environment such as noise, heat and toxic chemicals, which influence important needs and values both perceptually as well as objectively (Schuler, 1980; Beehr and Schuler, 1981).

This definition incorporates several important aspects of stress:

1. Stress can be positive (an opportunity) or negative (a constraint or demand). For example, a promotion can be perceived as a positive stress if the employee thinks that the promotion will lead to valued outcomes but is unsure about whether he or she can succeed or not. An example of negative stress is where an individual perceives he or she has a job that is really meaningless and really wants to get out of the situation (because he or she cannot satisfy any important values) but is not sure how.

2. Stress results from the transaction of the person and the environment (see Lazarus, 1978, for a discussion of the differences between viewing the person–environment as a transaction versus an interaction). The environment presents dynamic conditions (potential stressors) which can be perceived as opportunities, constraints or demands and which have perceived levels of uncertainty of resolution, and which have important outcomes. But what is important to one person may not be important to another because they may have different needs and values. The needs and values on which individuals can differ (at least in degree) are: certainty/predictability; achievement; recognition/acceptance; meaningfulness; responsibility; knowledge of results; fairness; variety/stimulation; safety/security; self-esteem; and physiological needs, such as food, water, physical safety, warmth and physical stimulation (see Locke, 1976; Cox, 1978; Schuler, 1980 for a more extensive review and discussion of these).

3. Stress can be associated with physical conditions as well as sociopsychological conditions. The stress associated with the physical conditions, however, is less perceptual than that associated with the sociopsychological conditions. Nevertheless perceptions of certain physical conditions are extremely critical in the level of stress they may elicit, for example, spatial relationships and safety conditions. Thus the dynamic state of demand is used to refer to physical conditions related to stress such as heat, light and noise, and the dynamic state of opportunity and constraint refers to sociopsychological conditions.

4. Stress is an additive concept across situations and over time. The more events in the organization perceived as stressful, the more stress experienced (Theorell, 1978). Holmes and Rahe (1967) found that individuals with the more severe illnesses had experienced more stressful events in the months preceding their illnesses than individuals with fewer severe illnesses. In addition to their study indicating the importance of the accumulation of stressful events over time, it also supported the notion that both positive (getting a new job) as well as negative events (losing one's job) can be associated with stress. Making both these types of events stressful are the uncertainty, the importance and the desire for resolution associated with them.

5. Stress and the desire for resolution are precipitated by events which cause a disruption of homeostasis, either physiological or psychological. Demand conditions in the environment disrupt physiological homeostasis and the body involuntarily seeks to restore homeostasis. A classical explanation of stress, for example, is that under the conditions of physical threat the body produces increased blood sugar, adrenaline and noradrenaline to help the individual in removing the physical threat (by providing the energy for either a "flight or fight response"; Cannon, 1979). The physical activity of the flight or fight response then utilizes the stress-produced physiological responses and the body is restored to homeostasis. Unfortunately, for constraint or opportunity stress associated with sociophysiological stress conditions, the body also responds involuntarily with the similar physiological reactions as with the physical stress conditions. In this case, however, it is less likely that the increased blood sugar, adrenaline and noradrenaline will be utilized through any physical exertion to restore the sociopsychological disequilibrium caused by the situation of opportunity or constraint. If other strategies for dealing with the stress are not utilized, long run wear and tear on the body will occur as the body fights to restore physiological homeostasis resulting in diseases of adaptation (Selye, 1956).

Thus stress is a perceived, dynamic state of uncertainty about something important to the individual. It can be both positive and negative. Most importantly, however, it is a dynamic condition most individuals seek to avoid, resolve or take advantage of (especially if it is a positive stress condition). Putting this definition in the context of a model of stress will help further elaborate each of these aspects of stress in organizations.

Integrative Transactional Process Model of Stress in Organizations

A model of stress in organizations is important not only because it provides an understanding of what stressors exist in an organization and how they work, but also because it shows what the outcomes of stress are, and what and where qualities of individuals influence their stress in organizations. Why an integrative transactional process model?

Transactional indicates that the relationships shown in the model are not linear but rather reciprocal. An individual experiences stress from his or her perception of the environment with his or her own set of unique skills, needs and characteristics. Thus, what is a stressor for one person may not be for another. An individual's response to the stress may alleviate the stress or provoke even more stress. Thus it is important to treat the components of the stress model as having multidirectional causation between them so that all components can be viewed as either causes or effects (Lazarus, 1978).

Process refers to what happens over time or across stressors. It contains two elements: (1) the actual interchange between the person and the environment (full of potential stressors) and (2) the person's responses over time to the stress experienced. Thus stress is not just a dynamic situation of importance involving uncertainty, but one which evokes individual responses which occur over time. The model is referred to as integrative since it has been developed from the literature and research in several, diverse areas and because a study of stress requires an interdisciplinary team.

The components of the transactional process model are the environmental stressors, individual characteristics and individual responses. Individual characteristics include those which influence the primary appraisal process an individual makes of the environment (to determine if there are stressors) and those which influence an individual's short-term, intermediate- and long-term responses. Responses are categorized into physiological, psychological and behavioral. An illustration of these components is shown in figure 6–1.

Organizational Stressors

There are seven major categories of potential stressors in organizations. Within each of these categories are several specific conditions or aspects of organizations which have been or can be related to stress as defined in this chapter (see Cooper and Marshall, 1976; Beehr and Newman, 1978; Schuler, 1980 and Brief, Schuler, and Van Sell, 1981 for a more complete description of these stressors). As such they are referred to as stressors. Although all of these stressors are crucial in understanding stress in organizations, space limitations permit only a discussion of a few.

As shown in figure 6–1 the stressors include physical conditions but the primary ones are the sociopsychological conditions. As noted earlier the impact of the physical conditions such as heat, light and noise, although significant for an individual's stress (Cooper and Marshall, 1976; Cox, 1978; Shostak, 1980), is probably less subject to an individual's subjective perception and interpretation than are the sociopsychological conditions. Consequently they are usually the province of industrial toxicology, environmental physiology and ergonomics (Kasl, 1978). Nonetheless, physical conditions can constitute an im-

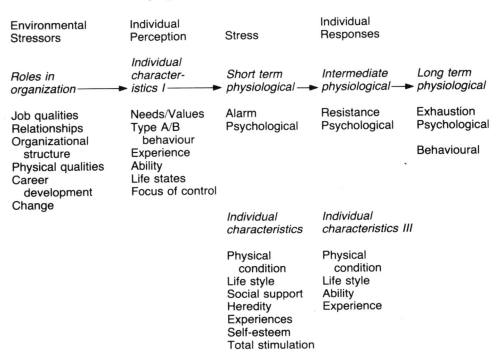

Figure 6–1. Integrative transactional process model of stress in organizations. Adapted from Schuler (1981).

portant stressor (Shostak, 1980; Cohen, 1980). Thus in the case of the sociopsychological conditions, the individual perceives the condition (primary appraisal), then interprets and evaluates (Lazarus, 1966) it *vis-à-vis* his or her desires (which are a reflection of his or her needs and values). To the extent it is perceived as disrupting a sociopsychological homeostasis (preventing a need/value from being fulfilled or offering the potential for fulfilling an important need/value) and, therefore, creating a desire for restoration of equilibrium and to the extent the restoration or resolution (though uncertain) will result in important outcomes, the condition becomes a stressor (McGrath, 1976). Between the stressor and the individual perception relationship and between the individual perception and stress relationship are the potential effects of several individual characteristics.

The organizational conditions most frequently identified and researched as stressors are job qualities, roles in the organizations and relationships at work. The job qualities commonly associated with stress are *work underload and work overload* (both qualitative and quantitative), although only limited research exists regarding underload. Overload or having too many things to do is associated with what Selye (1956) called hyperstress while underload is associated with hypostress.

French et al. (1974) indicate that at least nine different psychological and physiological responses have been found to be associated with qualitative and quantitative overload: job dissatisfaction, job tension, lower self-esteem, threat, embarrassment, high cholesterol levels, increased heart rate, skin resistance and increased smoking. Qualitative overload is a condition where the individual has job duties to perform which appear to exceed his or her abilities. This, of course, if compatible with our definition of stress just as is qualitative underload, which is a condition which may not supply enough needs to the individual. Quantitative overload is a condition of having too many job demands. With either overload condition it is likely that the individual becomes uncertain about whether or not he or she can meet all the job demands. In either case of underload the individual may desire to have more needs satisfied but is uncertain about how to change the current situation. There appear to be several needs not satisfied by either underload or overload conditions, particularly challenge, meaningfulness and self-control.

The two qualities of roles in the organization which have been widely researched are *role conflict* and *role ambiguity* (Van Sell, Brief, and Schuler, 1981). Role conflict is a potential stressor because it may prohibit an individual from doing well in all roles, or at least cause uncertainty about whether that is possible. Simlarly, role ambiguity may also prohibit an individual from experiencing a sense of accomplishment because the individual is *unclear* about what to accomplish.

Relationships with supervisors are often stressors for individuals in organizations. "Two major subjective stresses that blue-collarites associate with supervision involve the enervating pettiness of various work rules and the enervating nature of relentless pressure for more and more production" (Shostak, 1980). In either case, however, the individual is denied the fulfillment of a need to control as well as the needs for recognition and acceptance as an individual. As a result, individuals try to bend or violate rules—in essence regaining some control of their work situation.

These organizational stressors reviewed tend to be among the most common stressors in organizations. For example, the most common sources of stress for a sample of 5000 managers included inadequate support by supervisors, ineffective performance by supervisors, and conflict and ambiguity about what is expected (Pearse, 1977). All of these stressors are associated with many important needs of individuals and they are often uncertain how to deal with them.

Individual Characteristics I

The individual characteristics shown in figure 6–1 are needs and values, Type A/B behaviors, experience, ability, life stages, and locus of control. Although an individual's needs and values may influence what he or she perceives, the major influences of needs and values is on the individual's evaluation of the organizational conditions as causing a lack of fit between what needs and values of the individual the environment supplies and what needs and values the individual has. This evaluation is the essence of Lazarus's primary appraisal (1978).

Also influencing how an individual perceives the environment are the qualities of an individual's behavior or personality as being either Type A or Type B (Friedman and Rosenman, 1974; Gastorf, Suls, and Sanders, 1980). The qualities of Type B personality are held to be the opposite of Type A personality. As a result of the qualities of the Type A, he or she is more likely to perceive more stressors in the same environment than a Type B, as well as experience more situations with potential stressors than a Type B.

Type A behavior characteristics of individuals have been shown to increase the likelihood of coronary heart disease (Friedman and Rosenman, 1974). Consistent with this conceptualization, is the finding by Caplan and Jones (1975) that Type A behavior moderated the relationship between workload and anxiety. That is, Type A's reported a higher relationship between their perception of workload and anxiety than Type B's. Although this could be accounted for by the fact that the Type A may have perceived the level of workload as higher than Type B, it could as well be explained by the fact that the Type A interpreted the condition as more stressful. Since Type A's desire to get many things done and generally be in control, a high workload may likely be perceived as reducing one's probability (or increasing one's uncertainty) of getting things done.

Individual characteristics also enter the conceptualization of stress between the stress and the individual's short-term responses to the stress. These will be examined after discussing the short-term individual responses to stress.

Individual Responses: Short Term

The short-term individual responses are of two types: those physiological effects which occur immediately after the individual's perception of the stress and those psychological responses which also occur immediately after stress is perceived. The physiological effects which occur at this point (which corresponds to Selye's alarm stage) are increased blood and urine catecholamines (adrenaline and noradrenaline) and corticosteroids, increased blood glucose levels and increased heart rate and blood pressure (Selye, 1956). Whereas the short-term physiological effects occur regardless of the type of stress (opportunity, constraint or demand), the short-term psychological effects depend on the type of stress. Associated with the stress from situations of opportunity are psychological symptoms such as excitement, joy, high self-esteem and irritability from the stress associated with constraint and, to a lesser extent, demand situations. Regardless of the type of stress, however, there is the tendency to become forgetful, disorganized and impatient, and to block out information. The psychological reactions at this stage precede those which are a part of Lazarus's secondary appraisal where decisions are made about what to do. At this stage psychological reponses are more affective while at the intermediate stage they are more cognitive.

Individual Characteristics II

The degree of severity of the short term physiological responses is moderated by all seven characteristics shown in the Individual characteristics II box in figure 6-1. Individuals respond physiologically with less severity, that is, less increased blood and urine catecholamines, to a stress situation when they are in good physical condition, have fewer life changes, have socially supportive relationships, are hereditarily strong, have had many experiences with stress (and therefore developed what amounts to immunity), have high self-esteem and have a moderate level of total stimulation than individuals with the opposite characteristics. (Brief, Schuler, and Van Sell, 1981; House, 1981). Individuals who have socially supportive relationships are more physiologically capable of dealing with stress because of the acceptance shown by others and the awareness of those who can and will help if and when needed (Klein, 1971; House, 1981).

House and Wells (1978) have concluded that under maximum levels of social support, symptoms of ill health increase only slightly, if at all, as stressors increase. Yet when social support is low, with increasing stress, symptoms of ill health are high (McLean, 1979). Social support groups appear to aid individuals in dealing with stress by conditioning or buffering the individuals to the effects of stress. Social support groups can also aid individuals in a much more active way as well, for instance by helping to reduce role conflict or role ambiguity.

Individual Responses: Intermediate Term

If the short physiological responses to stress are not utilized, for example in a flight or fight response, the body will seek to restore equilibrium. The body in Selye's term enters a stage of resistance or adaptation, seeking to diminish or resist the initial physiological responses of the alarm stage. But as a consequence of this process, the body suffers from "diseases of adaptation." During this stage the body's immune system becomes less effective. These diseases include asthma, chest and back pains, faintness and dizziness, migraines, neuroses, insomnia, nightmares, psychoses and skin rash (Selye, 1956; Cox, 1978).

At this intermediate stage (which also can be conceived of as the secondary appraisal or coping stage), the individual's primary psychological response is deciding what to do. Although laden with the short-term psychological responses which may include tendencies to be disorganized and forgetful as well as to block out potentially useful information from the environment, the individual will decide to engage in one of four modes of coping: information seeking, direct action, inhibition of action and intraphychic processes (Lazarus, 1978). These will be discussed further in the section on coping strategies.

Individual Characteristics III

The severity and the type of the intermediate physiological responses of stress are influenced by the individual's physical conditions, life style, heredity, problem solving skill, ability, social support network and experiences. These characteristics, as shown in figure 6–1, also influence an individual's long-term physiological responses. Life-style qualities which aid in reducing an individual's likelihood of incurring severe disease of this stage include (1) a diet of low fat and low cholesterol; (2) no smoking; (3) moderate drinking; and (4) regular exercise two to three times a week. Again an individual's heredity, particularly as related to a history of hypertension and coronary heart disease, social support networks, and experiences have the same moderating effect here as they do with short-term responses.

Individual Responses: Long Term

To this set of responses is added the behavioral category. Although there are behaviors associated with the implementation of the active

strategies, those behaviors are more a function of the individual's intermediate term psychological reaction than they are of stress. As shown
in the figure, however, the implementation of a strategy influences the
long-term behavioral responses, as well as the psychological and physiological responses, of the individual. But this influence occurs regardless of the strategy used. Consequently the long-term behavior
responses presented here are associated with stress in organizations.

A major set of individual behavioural responses has immediate
implication for organizational effectiveness. The direction of the responses, however, depends on the type of stress. Negatively associated
with opportunity stress are employee turnover and absenteeism and
positively associated with opportunity stress is the quantity of performance, especially on tasks the employee knows how to do. The relationship between opportunity stress and quality of performance is
curvilinear, with quality being higher at moderate levels of stress (see
McGrath, 1976; Schuler, 1980 for a more extensive discussion). Stress
associated with demand and constraint situations on the other hand is
negatively related to both aspects of performance and positively related
to employee turnover and absenteeism.

The long-term psychological responses of an individual are also
dependent on the type of stress. With increased opportunity stress are
associated *higher* levels of employee satisfaction, involvement, sense
of responsibility, self-esteem and sense of challenge and accomplishment, and also tension and anxiety. But with increased constraint or
demand stress are *lower* levels of these same psychological responses
as well as with feelings of tension and anxiety. It is at this point that
dissatisfaction is likely to feedback and appear to cause even more
stress as House (1974) reported. To the extent, however, that the individual can implement an effective strategy to cope with the constraint
or demand stress, these essentially negative psychological responses
can be minimized. The same is true for the physiological responses.

Although the individual's psychological and behavioral responses
are influenced by the type of stress, as indicated with short term and
intermediate term conditions, physiological responses are the same regardless of the source of stress. This stage of long term physiological
responses could be depicted as Selye's (1956) exhaustion stage.

Thus the integrative process transactional model of stress in organizations has several important features. First, it identifies stress and
its associated symptoms as a process that is not only perceptual but
also takes place over time. Secondly, several individual characteristics
critical during the times over which the symptoms of stress unfold are

incorporated into the model. And thirdly, several organizational conditions are discussed and incorporated into the model. These three aspects are critical because they help show how individuals may be effective in dealing with stress and the benefits for doing so.

Strategies to Deal with Stress

Individual Strategies

Stressors and stress in organizations evoke different reactions from different people. "Some people are better able to cope with these stressors than others, they adapt their behaviour in a way that meets the environmental challenge. On the other hand, some people are more characterologically predisposed to stress, that is, they are unable to cope or adapt to the stress-provoking situation" (Cooper and Marshall, 1976, pp. 22–23). Coping strategies individuals can use are defined by Lazarus and his colleagues as information-seeking, direct action, inhibition of action, and intrapsychic processes. People who are better at coping probably use the most appropriate strategy given the stress-provoking situation.

Coping through *information-seeking* can encompass a wide range of resulting actions. In this cognitive strategy, knowledge is sought to make a sound coping decision. This is essentially a problem-solving strategy. This strategy enables the individual to reduce uncertainty that exists regarding resolution of the stressful condition. Ability to seek out information related to the stress condition often takes place at the intermediate response stage.

"Anything one does (except cognitively) to handle stressful transactions falls within the rubric of *direct action*" (Lazarus, 1978, p. 37). This can include exercising, engaging in time mamagement activities, altering the environmental stressors, and even fleeing from the stressors. The appropriateness of the direct action is often determined by the conditions associated with the stress. For example, action to try to change the behavior of an ineffective supervisor many not only meet with a lack of success but is likely to result in even more stress. As a consequence of implementing this type of direct action, the individual will evaluate the results. On this basis, the individual may engage in a longer-term behavioral strategy such as absenteeism.

Faced with a generally unmovable stressor, direct action away from the stressor is more likely to be successful than one aimed at the stressor. Direct action, however, is only one way an individual can cope with an ineffective supervisor.

Intrapsychic modes of coping are often used by individuals in organizations. A common one is through the reduction in the importance of what's at stake. Individuals faced with ineffective supervisors may reduce the importance of good supervisors or of doing good work. Consequently, individuals may appear lethargic, uninvolved and alienated. Contrary to being preferred feelings, these are merely means of coping. Typical expression of intrapsychic coping include "Forget about it," "Don't worry, everything will be all right" and "It's really not that important."

A final mode of coping is the *inhibition of action*. Often it is best when faced with a stressor to hold back action impulses that will do harm rather than take action that poorly fits the requirement of the situation. Although an individual may be frustrated with an ineffective supervisor, expressing anger at work, being absent from work, or reducing the importance may not be reasonable or discrete modes of coping. A typical saying related to inhibition of action is "Grin and bear it."

Although these modes of coping were discussed separately, in reality they are difficult to untangle, as individuals often use several modes concurrently. Nevertheless Folkman and Lazarus (1980), using extensive interviewing, reported that different modes are associated with different situational stressors. For example they reported that work-related stressors generated increased problem-focused coping, and personal and family-related stressors generated intrapsychic, emotion-focused coping. Thus, whether an individual is effective at coping or not may depend upon his/her ability to accurately perceive the stressor and determine the appropriate response, including generating alternative strategies, implementing the best one and evaluating the implemented strategy.

Although several hypotheses about individual stress in organizations have been implied, it is critical to present them explicitly. Only in this way can the definition and conceptualization of stress developed here be appropriately tested.

Testable Research Hypotheses

Based upon the definition of stress and the integrative transactional process model of stress presented here several hypotheses are proposed:

1. The intensity of a stress condition, whether demand, constraint or opportunity, is determined by the perceived importance of the situation and the respective uncertainty attached to the condition itself and the resolution of the condition.

This proposition is consistent with most of the stress literature which even suggests that without important outcomes at stake there is not stress (Sells, 1970). Furthermore, as the number of outcomes and their associated uncertainty and importance attached to each type of stress associated with a dynamic condition increases, the more stress an individual will experience from that condition.

2. Stress is associated with three groups of symptoms: physiological, psychological and behavioral. The occurrence of these symptoms will take place in the short term, intermediate and long term.

These stress–stress symptom relationships need to be examined by type of stress and by type of symptom. Below are some tentative associations between types of symptoms.

2a. Opportunity, constraint and demand stresses are all positively related to the probability of the incidence of physiological symptoms.

Although the limited non-organizational stress research suggests that even *certain* physiological symptoms may not always occur with stress, it is felt that evidence does not warrant propositions between types of stresses and *specific* physiological symptoms. Furthermore, the data do not even allow specification of relationships among the physiological symptoms, for instance that increased blood pressure precedes CHD.

2b. Demand stress, constraint stress, and opportunity stress are positively related to cognitive psychological outcomes such that the higher of any of these stress types, the greater an individual's perceptual distortion, tunnel vision, and tendency to misjudge others.

2c. Opportunity stress is positively related to affective psychological outcomes such as satisfaction and job involvement.

The opportunity to gain valued outcomes, to fulfill one's needs and values, should be associated with satisfaction and job involvement (Locke, 1976).

2d. Opportunity stress is negatively related to some behavioral symptoms such as absenteeism and turnover.

Under opportunity stress the individual has the potential to gain more of what he or she desires. The potential, however, can be experienced and realized only when the individual engages in the behavior, that is, stays with the organization in which the opportunity stress is experienced.

2e. Opportunity stress and the constraint stress have an inverted U relationship with some behavioral symptoms such as performance. The relationships are influenced by the nature of the task and performance criterion such that:

(1) The apex of the inverted U is higher under an easy task and/or

with a quantity measure of performance. In addition, under these conditions, the right half of the inverted U declines very little.

(2) The apex of the inverted U is lower under a difficult task and/or with a quality measure of performance.

2f. Demand stress in negatively related to some behavioral symptoms such as performance.

Propositions 2e and 2f, although not explicated as such in the previous literature and research, are generally consistent with Sales (1969), Levi (1972), McGrath (1976), Gal and Lazarus (1975) and Anderson (1976). In proposition 2e, it is suggested that an individual wants to and will perform to take advantage of the stress-related opportunity or to try to overcome the stress-related constraint. Increased performance is facilitated by an easy task and/or a quantity measure of performance. This increase, however, can occur only to a point because of the increased arousal level (Scott, 1966). If the task is difficult, problem-solving behavior is required to perform well, and as Anderson (1976) reported, problem-solving declines with increased stress; therefore, performance will decline. With demand stress, an individual's physical ability to peform is impaired and thus, regardless of task type of performance measure, will perform less well with increasing demand stress (see Cohen, 1980, for a discussion of related issues).

3. Individuals who engage in the process of gathering information, generating alternatives, selecting and implementing an alternative, and finally evaluating the implemented strategy will be more effective and efficient at coping with stress than individuals who do not take this methodical approach to coping.

Partial support for this hypothesis is based on the work of Howard, Rechnitzer and Cunningham (1975); Antonovsky (1979); Lazarus (1978) and Gal and Lazarus (1975) which suggests that when individuals are more methodical in their analysis of a stressful situation they are more likely to produce a wider range of potentially effective coping strategies than if they do not. This in conjunction with Anderson's (1976) findings suggesting that individuals should try to avoid situations in which they are facing too much stress since this may preclude a problem-solving approach to coping strategies.

4. The efficacy of coping strategies is dependent upon the situation.

A strategy to change the situation when the situation *is not* likely to change will be less successful than if the situation *is* likely to change. In fact, it is likely that more stress will result if the inappropriate strategy is chosen than if none is chosen. Thus, it is important to be able to analyze stress situations and successfully identify the realistic constraints. In addition to the identification, it is necessary to develop a repertoire of strategies, applicable to changing the organization or the individual, which can be matched and evaluated with different stressful situations. A consequence of this matching and testing may be a contingency or situational approach to coping. Fortunately some current research suggests that a contingency approach may not only be an effective and efficient way of coping, but in fact what individuals do, at least those who are successful (see, for example, the work by Folkman and Lazarus, 1980; Jackson and Maslack, 1980).

These third and fourth hypotheses imply that for an individual to engage in effective coping he or she must be not only perceptive but adaptable as well. Thus making individuals aware of this cognitive–diagnostic approach to coping strategies will not insure that they will actually select or implement the most effective strategy. But even if individuals are completely adaptable, it is still likely that individuals would not select the most effective strategy. Because of time and information processing capabilities it is more probable to suspect that individuals will select a coping strategy which at least produces a satisfactory resolution (Simon, 1976). This is especially likely to occur under conditions where individuals find it necessary to develop strategies for several stressful conditions.

5. Individuals who possess good problem-solving and decision-making skills will produce more effective coping strategies than those who do not.

There are individual differences in problem-solving and decision-making skills (Driver and Streufert, 1969; Milburn, 1981). In addition, individuals high in these skills will be more likely to diagnose and analyze stressful conditions more effectively than individuals low in these skills. Such being the case, individuals who are high in these skills will also be more likely to select more effective coping strategies than individuals low in these skills.

Conclusion

Stress in organizations is becoming an increasingly important concern in organizations because of its potentially severe detrimental effects. In order to effectively deal with stress and its effects it is important to know what it is and the processes by which it produces the detrimental effects. In this chapter a definition and model of stress were presented in order to facilitate understanding and dealing with stress. To illustrate how the definition and model of stress help in dealing with stress, individual and organizational strategies were briefly reviewed. These were anchored in the definition and model. Presently many of the relationships depicted in the model of stress are relatively unexamined.

Thus, research is necessary. Suggestions for future research were offered in terms of several hypotheses based upon the definition and model of stress presented.

Research focused on the hypotheses suggested here is necessary in order to advance our understanding of stress and the way individuals can cope with stress. Although this chapter has addressed a specific definition and conceptualization of stress, it is imperative that neither this nor any other single definition and conceptualization of stress drive all the stress research. This is because of the relative infancy of systematic stress in organizations research, and it would be premature to foreclose other approaches to individual stress that in fact may prove to be more effective.

References

Anderson, D.R. (1976). Coping behaviours as intervening mechanisms in the inverted-U-stress performance relationship. *Journal of Applied Psychology, 61,* 30–34.

Antonovsky, A. (1969). *Health, Stress and Coping.* San Francisco, Jossey–Bass.

Beehr, T.A. and Newman, J.E. (1978). Job stress, employee health, and organizational effectiveness: A facet analysis, model and literature review. *Personal Psychology, 31,* 665–699.

Beehr, T.A., and Schuler, R.S. (1981). Current and future perspectives on stress in organizations. In Rowland and Ferris (Eds.) *Personnel Management: New Perspectives.* Boston, Allyn and Bacon.

Brief, A.P., Schuler, R.S. and Van Sell, M. (1981). *Managing Stress.* Boston, Little, Brown.

Cameron, C. (1971). Fatigue problems in modern industry. *Ergonomics, 14,* 713–718.

Cannon, W.B. (1979). Organization for physiological homeostasis. *Physiological Review, 9,* 339–340.

Caplan, R.D., Cobb, S. and French, J.R.P. (1975). Relationships of cessation of smoking with job stress, personality and social support. *Journal of Applied Psychology, 60,* 211–219.

Caplan, R.D. and Jones, K.W. (1975). Effects of workload, role ambiguity and Type A personality on anxiety, depression and heart rate. *Journal of Applied Psychology, 60,* 713–719.

Coch, L. and French, J.R.P. (1948). Overcoming resistance to change. *Human Relations, 11,* 512–532.

Cohen, S. (1980). Aftereffects of stress on human performance and social behaviour: A review of research and theory. *Psychology Bulletin, 88,* 82–108.

Cooper, C.L. and Marshall, J. (1976). Occupational sources of stress: A review of the literature relating to coronary heart disease and mental ill health. *Journal of Occupational Psychology, 49,* 11–28.

Cooper, C.L. and Payne, R. (Eds.) (1978). *Stress at Work.* Wiley, New York.

Cooper, C.L. and Payne, R. (1979). *Current Concerns in Occupational Stress.* Wiley, New York.

Cox, T. (1978). *Stress.* University Park Press, Baltimore.

Drabek, T.E. and Haas, J.E. (1969). Laboratory simulation of organizational stress. *American Sociological Review, 34,* 223–238.

Driver, M. and Streufert, S. (1969). Integrative complexity: An approach to individuals and groups as information-processing systems. *Administrative Science Quarterly, 12,* 272–285.

Folkman, S. and Lazarus, R.W. (1980). An analysis of coping in a middle-aged community sample. *Journal of Health and Social Behaviour.*

French, J.R.P., Jr., Rogers, W. and Cobb, S. (1974). Adjustment as a person environment fit. In: Coelho, G.V., Hamburg, D.A., and Adams, J.F. (Eds.) *Coping and Adaptation: Interdisciplinary Perspectives.* Basic Book, New York.

Friedman, M. and Rosenman, R.H. (1974). *Type A Behavior and Your Heart.* Fawcett Pulbications, Inc., Greenwich, Conn.

Galbraith, J. (1977). *Organization Design.* Addison-Wesley, Reading, Ma.

Gastorf, J.W., Suls, J. and Sanders, G.S. (1980). Type A coronary-prone behaviour pattern and social facilitation. *Journal of Personality and Social Psychology, 38,* 773–780.

Gal, R. and Lazarus, R.W. (1975). The role of activity in anticipating and confronting stressful situations. *Journal of Human Stress, 2,* 4–20.

Greenwood, J.W. (1978). Management stressors. In: *Reducing Occupational Stress.* NIOSH Research Report, Cincinnati.

Harvey, D.F. (1970). Cross-cultural stress and adaptation in global organizations. Doctoral dissertation, Case Western Reserve University, 1969. *Dissertation Abstracts International, 31,* 2958B. (University Microfilms, No. 70–4931.)

Holmes, T.H. and Rahe, R.H. (1967). Social readjustment rating scale. *Journal of Psychomatic Research, 11,* 213–218.

House, J.S. (1974). Occupational stress and coronary heart disease: A review and theoretical integration. *Journal of Health and Social Behaviour, 15,* 12–27.

————. (1981). *Social Support and Stress.* Addison-Wesley Publishing Co., Reading, Ma.

House, J.S., and Wells, J.A. (1978). Occupational stress and health. In: *Reducing Occupational Stress.* NIOSH Research Report, Cincinnati.

Howard, J.H., Rechnitzer, P.A. and Cunningham, D.A. (1975). Coping with job tensions-effective methods. *Public Personnel Management, 1,* 317–326.

Jackson S.E. and Maslack, C. (1980). Job stress among helping professionals: The effects on workers and their families. Paper presented at York University.

Jacobson, D. (1972). Fatigue-producing factors in industrial work and preretirement attitude. *Occupational Psychology, 46,* 193–200.

Kasl, S.V. (1978). Epidemiological contributors to the study of work stress. In: Cooper, C.L., and Payne, R. *Stress at Work.* Wiley, New York.

Klein, S.M. (1971). *Workers Under Stress.* University Press of Kentucky, Lexington.

Lazarus, R.S. (1966). *Psychological Stress and the Coping Process.* McGraw-Hill, New York.

————. (1978). The stress and coping paradigm. Paper presented at Glendon Beach, Oregon, November 3–6.

Levi, T. (1972). *Stress and Distress in Response to Psychosocial Stimuli.* Pergamon Press, Inc., Elmsford, N.Y.

Locke, E.A. (1976). The nature and causes of job satisfaction. In: Dunnette, M.D. (Ed.) *Handbook of Industrial and Organizational Psychology.* Rand McNally College, Chicago.

Matteson, M.T. and Ivancevich, J.M. (1979). Organizational stressors and heart disease: A research model. *Academy of Management Review, 4,* 347–358.

McGrath, J.E. (1976). Stress and behaviour in organizations. In: Dunnette, M.D. (Ed.) *Handbook of Industrial and Organizational Psychology.* Rand McNally College Publishing Company, Chicago.

McLean, A.A. (1979). *Work stress.* Addison-Wesley Publishing Company, Reading, Ma.

Milburn, T.W. (1981). Maximizing degrees of freedom over time as a principal of rational behaviour. Working paper, the Ohio State University.

Newman, J.F. and Beehr, T.A. (1979). Personal and Organizational strategies for handling job stress: A review of research and opinion. *Personnel Psychology, 32,* 1–43.

Pearse, R. (1977). *What Managers Think About their Managerial Careers,* AMACOM, New York.

Sales, S.M. (1969). Organizational roles as a risk factor in coronary heart disease. *Administrative Science Quarterly, 14,* 325–336.

Schuler, R.S. (1980). Definition and conceptualization of stress in organizations. *Organizational Behaviour and Human Performance, 24,* 115–130.

Sells, S.B. (1970). On the nature of stress. In: McGrath, J.E. (Ed.) *Social and Psychological Factors in Stress.* Holt Rinehart, New York.

Selye, H. (1956). *The Stress of Life.* McGraw-Hill Book Co., New York.

Shostak, A.B. (1980). *Blue Collar Stress.* Addison-Wesley Publishing Company, Reading, Ma.

Theorell, T. (1978). Workload, life change and myocardial infarction. In: *Reducing Occupational Stress.* NIOSH Research Report, Cincinnati.

Van Sell, M., Brief, A.P. and Schuler, R.S. (1981). Role conflict and role ambiguity: Integration of the literature and directions for future research. *Human Relations, 34,* 43–71.

Warshaw, L.J. (1979). *Stress Management.* Addison-Wesley Publishing Company, Reading, Ma.

Industrial and Organizational Psychology Perspective on Productivity Research

Benjamin Schneider

This chapter focuses on a set of topics traditionally associated with Industrial and Organizational (I/O) Psychology, including criterion development, personnel selection, training, work motivation, and job satisfaction. Leadership and group behavior will only be mentioned in passing, although they are traditionally thought of as in the I/O domain of interest. Of course the theory and research on leadership and groups comprises a large portion of the "O" in I/O and most of the newer field of Organizational Behavior. Be that as it may, because it is obvious that a brief chapter by one person can only hint at some of the ideas and approaches of a field as wide-ranging and dynamic as I/O, no caveats are presented.

The chapter outline will be in the order just mentioned. The first item, criterion development, concerns the uniqueness of I/O's approach, that is, its concern for performance and other important organizational outcomes (called criteria) through a focus on individual attributes and behavior.

I/O Psychology: The Focus on Performance Criteria

I/O Psychology is an approach to understanding organizational functioning and effectiveness via an understanding of relationships between individual attributes and individual job behavior. The hallmark of I/O has been a concern for establishing empirical and theoretical relationships between various individual characteristics (abilities, needs, satisfactions) and the organization-relevant behaviors (output, turnover) of those same individuals. Implicitly, then, I/O is based on the simple assumption that if one can make accurate predictions about the effectiveness of individuals one and takes action based on those predictions, then it follows that the organization will be more effective. For example, I/O researchers assume that if it is shown that assessments of individuals at the time of hire are significantly related to criteria on

Reprinted from Arthur P. Brief (ed.), *Productivity Research in the Behavioral and Social Sciences*. New York: Praeger Publishers, © 1984. Reprinted with permission.

the job two or five or ten years later, then utilization of the assessment technique for hiring people will yield a higher proportion of effective workers and the organization will be more effective.

Almost every topic to be discussed in this chapter has this focus on relationships and effectiveness. This emphasis seems to have evolved from I/O's emergence from Functional Psychology and its dedication to understanding the function or utility of individual attributes and behavior (Boring, 1950). This orientation (the same one that produced the psychometric movement in education) resulted in psychologists from academe being able to design procedures useful in making decisions about military recruits. After World War I, some of the useful assessment procedures that were developed proved valuable in both education and industry. While some progress in the basic test validation model was made between the Wars, (cf. Viteles, 1932) it was in World War II that what has become contemporary I/O Psychology really proved its worth.

During World War II, psychologists were recruited to conduct research regarding all kinds of human functioning. The topics ranged from team morale to selecting pilots and from psychological warfare to dealing with pilot errors. Psychologists and their methods proved themselves. Given a problem to which they could apply the model of establishing relationships, psychologists were able to produce results: they improved team morale, they selected better pilots, they produced strategies for debriefing POWs, and they designed equipment so that human errors were reduced.

The method they used, indeed still use, was to focus on the criterion (the dependent variable). That is, in all the problems they faced, the first thing the psychologists learned to do was to operationalize what was to be understood and predicted, or at least predicted. They learned that descriptions of people and their attributes, or of training programs for squads, was vacuous in the absence of something to which those descriptions could be related. They learned that only when a relationship between assessments and an important criterion was established did one know which descriptions were important for performance and which to discount as mere armchair theorizing. This focus on important organization-relevant outcomes and the correlates of those outcomes has made I/O psychologists as a group quite anti-fad. They seem to have both the scientist's basic cynicism and a concern for practical criteria that promotes a focus on the requirement of evidence to support an assertion.

The most important outcome of the work by psychologists in the Second World War was a dedication to the reliable assessment of criteria. This focus on the reliability of the criterion permitted the growth and development of I/O Psychology and allowed its acceptance in business and industry. This happened because the focus on organizationally relevant criteria permitted I/O psychologists to demonstrate the utility of their approaches. While considerable progress has been made in criterion measurement and development since WWII, the fact is that the "criterion problem" has become the core idea in I/O Psychology, and it is around this core that all other topics take on their meaning. An outline of some of the contemporary issues comprising the criterion problem follows (for detailed discussions see Blum and Naylor, 1968; Landy and Trumbo, 1980; Smith, 1976).

The Criterion Problem

There are three fundamental issues regarding criteria: criterion relevance, criterion reliability, and job analysis. Each is an important topic; they interact with each other, so the order of presentation is a problem. From a conceptual standpoint, however, criterion relevance is the most important idea.

Criterion Relevance. This refers to the conceptual issue of the degree of overlap between what the ideal indicator of effectiveness would be and what actually is assessed and used as the index or indices. The ultimate criterion is obviously never obtained, so the relevance of any performance indicator that is used is a judgment.

Unfortunately, the criteria we choose to use for indexing performance are more often available or easily obtainable than they are relevant. For example, teller contribution to increases in customer deposits to a bank is never assessed, but a $20.00 shortage at the end of a day is grounds for teller dismissal. Thus, a focus on criteria that are easily countable rather than on criteria that may be more relevant to long-term organizational viability has characterized the thinking of management when choosing their performance standards. In this light, it is interesting to note that the automobile industry has chosen to report its ten-day car output as its major index of productivity. Not only is this a short-run index but it surely is not particularly relevant as a long-term index of organizational viability.

Sometimes people debate the subjectivity (ratings) or objectivity (production per hour) of criteria, but the more fundamental point is that the choice of criteria is a judgment. The actual choice process of what to try to predict or understand is rarely studied, nor is the reliability of the choice understood. So, for example, differences in the processes for organizations that emphasize quantity versus quality, or ratings of supervisory support versus goal-setting for subordinates, or turnover versus productivity, have not been studied. In addition, the importance attached to these criteria by different people in an organization (interrater reliability), or by the same people at different points in time (rerate reliability) has received little attention.

A failure to tie the actual criteria used by I/O psychologists to larger organizational issues, like the ability of the organization to adapt to turbulent environments, has resulted in some scholars questioning the utility of I/O with respect to long-term organizational viability (Argyris, 1976; Schneider, 1982). Thus, by accepting jobs and organizations as they exist, including accepting what organizations consider to be the important criteria to be predicted, it may be argued that I/O psychologists can facilitate the perpetuation of mediocrity. However, it may also be argued that application of the I/O focus on criteria leads to a class of decisions being made that at least contribute to what the organization (that is, the management of the organization) believes is in its long-term interest.

Regardless of I/O's role in this debate, it is clear that little of what is known about how organizations come to choose particular goals, how those goals are related to or reflected in particular organizational forms, how organizational forms are related to job design and, thus, how the standards of effectiveness for job incumbents are established has entered the I/O literature (for example, see Beer, 1980; Hage, 1980; Thompson, 1967). This stream of connections clearly requires attention if the criterion problem is to be addressed with long-term organizational viability as a concern.

Criterion Reliability. More frequently studied has been the reliability of the chosen criteria. This may be fortunate because some such seemingly objective criteria as unit turnover rates or bombardier accuracy may have poor reliability. For example, in life insurance agencies, the stability of turnover is low because high replacement rates one year yield low turnover the next; the *cycles* for criteria also need to be understood. Or, bombardier accuracy was shown to have stability (rerate reliability) as a function of numerous contaminants:: changes in weather, pilot, wind, and so forth from one bombing to another. The point here is that the stability of all criteria should be considered suspect until established to the contrary. Establishment to the contrary requires samples of data over time.

Interrater (agreement between raters) and internal consistency (homogeneity of facets) reliability become important when ratings are used as criteria. I/O psychologists over the years have established some excellent procedures for the development of reliable ratings, insuring these kinds of reliability (see Landy and Farr, 1980; Latham and Wexley, 1981). Most of these contemporary rating techniques focus on assessments of ratee behavior, and this focus appears to avoid or diminish many of the problems associated with ratings, specifically halo (focusing on one or two incidents that intrude all rated facets of performance), bias (in terms of sex, race, age, and so on), leniency, harshness, or central tendency (the tendency of a rater to put a large proportion of ratees in a similar place on the rating scale). Preparation of these Behaviorally Anchored Rating Scales (BARS) or Behavior Observations Scales (BOS) are based on job analysis, and I/O psychologists here, too, have made major contributions: these will be discussed below. However, here it is worth noting that in the absence of reliable job analysis procedures, the development of relevant and reliable performance rating systems is not possible.

As noted earlier, then, much more effort is required to tie the actual productivity of individuals on which we focus to the real long-term goals of the organization. This can obviously only happen when the management of organizations actually state goals in measurable terms so that the criteria actually assessed for any one job can be examined for their relevance to these more long-term goals. In truth, I/O psychologists have not pushed as hard on this issue as they should.

Criterion Dimensionality and Job Analysis. Jobs are multidimensional in their requirements for behavior. This means that all jobs incumbents to display a variety of (sometimes conflicting) behaviors for effectiveness. Given this fact, a single index of effectiveness, except at the most abstract level, is not useful. So, strategies have evolved for indexing the variety of behaviors effective workers must display. In brief, the maxim on I/O is to conduct a thorough job analysis and isolate the critical behaviors required for effectiveness.

I/O psychologists have made major contributions to job analysis technology, and job analysis lies at the root of all useful personnel procedures including criterion development, personnel selection, training and performance appraisal. Occasionally, some confusion exists about some terminology similar to job analysis but Landy and Trumbo (1980, p. 142) have clarified these:

> Job analysis, job evaluation, job description, and performance appraisal differ in some important respects. Job analysis is a process for identifying critical job elements that are most crucial for job success. Job evaluation is a process for placing a dollar value on those elements and assigning wage rates to jobs according to the number and involvement of the job elements identified in the job analysis. A job description is a listing of job duties based on the job analysis. Performance

appraisal concentrates on describing the job performance of a particular individual, rather than the characteristics of a job.

Contemporary job analysis procedures like Functional Job Analysis (FJA; Fine, 1974), the Position Analysis Questionnaire (PAQ;
McCormick, 1979) or the Critical Incidents Technique (CIT; cf. Fivars,
1975) focus on the kinds of behaviors job incumbents need to display
at work. As such, they translate relatively easily into behavior or performance *dimensions* that can then be used for appraisal purposes and
as a source of hypotheses (or hunches as Guion, 1965, calls them) for
designing selection and training programs.

It is important to note that dimensions of behavior are not the
same as output/productivity, like sales, or number of widgets produced, or amount of scrappage. These latter are *outcomes* of behavior.
Thus, I/O psychologists have tried to focus on the dimensions of behavior that *produce* output/productivity as well as on the outcomes
themselves. This attention to behavior, of course, facilitates the selection and training of people who are likely to be more rather than less
effective. That is, if one focuses only on overall effectiveness, a very
abstract idea, how a person is likely to be effective is difficult to specify
and so difficult to select for and train.

Summary

This brief survey of issues in "the criterion problem" is meant to suggest the progress I/O has made in focusing on worker performance and
effectiveness. Not only does a fairly sophisticated technology now exist
for assessing worker behavior, but the technology produces reliable,
relevant, and multidimensional views of performance behavior. In addition, recent conceptual work has yielded potentially important insights into some issues regarding the role of criterion relevance in I/O
research for long-term organizational viability. Researchers, then are
beginning to examine the role of individual level performance data so
that the part I/O can play in the prediction and understanding of organizational effectiveness may become more clear (Beer, 1980; Schneider, 1982). This issue will emerge again in the discussion of work
motivation.

Personnel Selection

The Basic Test-Validation Model

The personnel selection model is based on the individual differences
philosophy, that is, on the idea that people differ in their capacity and

willingness to behave and that those differences are reflected in their on-the-job behavior. By the end of World War II, the basic personnel selection validation model was known:

1. Job analysis to define the kinds of behaviors required by the job.
2. Develop the criteria for job performance that are going to be predicted.
3. Develop the predictors.
4. Establish relationship between predictors and criteria (validity).
5. Establish the utility of the predictors, that is, are they cost effective?

Especially when this selection validation model was used with large military samples it produced useful results. However, when used on small samples (say, less than 100 people) typically available for a validation study in industry, results varied from situation to situation even when the same predictors and criteria for seemingly the same job were used. This variability in validity was quite disconcerting and resulted in the admonishment to "revalidate in each new setting." Fortunately, Ghiselli (1966) produced a review of the validity of occupational tests that revealed that these tests were typically valid, and recently Schmidt and his colleagues (for example, Schmidt & Hunter, 1978, 1980) have shown that a substantial proportion of the variability in validity from setting to setting can be attributed to measurement problems such as unreliability of the criterion and small sample size. In other words, Ghiselli, and Schmidt and Hunter, have shown that the sampling distributions of validities for particular predictor-criterion relationships have stable averages that suggest the potential utility of predictors for a very broad range of job types and criteria; that there exists "validity generalization."

Indeed, from clerical performance to computer programming and from sales to management, there is no doubt about the predictability of performance at work using validated personnel selection procedures. But, great debate over this statement has existed for about 20 years, primarily driven by assertions that tests are unfair discriminators against minorities. While the past 10–15 years have been stormy ones regarding the validity and fairness of tests (see Arvey, 1980, for a review), and legal issues in selection have occupied many I/O Psychologists, recently a National Academy of Sciences Report (1982, p. 144) concluded that there was

> no evidence of alternatives to testing that are equally informative, equally adequate technically, and also economically and politically

viable . . . and little evidence that well-constructed and competently administered tests are more valid predictors for a population subgroup than for another: individuals with higher scores tend to perform better on the job regardless of group identity.

The report also added the note that the attack on testing seems to have been motivated by an attempt to redress *societal* issues by requiring tests to yield a proportionate work force: "The validity of the testing process should not be comprised in the effort to shape the distribution of the workforce" (p. 148).

Alternatives to Paper and Pencil Tests:
Interviews and Exercises

The typical predictor for I/O Psychologists has been the paper and pencil test. This is true for two very practical reasons: They work and they are inexpensive to administer. In contrast to the selection interview, for example, a roomful of applicants can be adminsitered a test while one applicant is being interviewed, and there is precious little evidence to support the validity of interviews, especially against typical job performance criteria (Schmitt, 1976; Tenopyr, 1981). Perhaps because every person thinks of him/herself as a psychologist, the interview is still the most frequently used selection procedure.

Interviews probably fail to yield significant validity coefficients for two reasons: They are unreliable in that two interviewers interviewing the same candidate will not agree; and attempts are made to validate interviews against inappropriate criteria like on-the-job performance. Interviews can be made more reliable: have the questions moderately to severely structured so that different interviewers are asking similar questions; train the interviewers to consider all the information they obtain from an applicant rather than making first-impression judgments; provide interviewers with some standards against which to judge an applicant's suitability (see Carlson, Thayer, Mayfield and Peterson, 1971; Schmitt, 1976).

Regarding which criteria interviews can predict, there is now some fairly good evidence to suggest that interviews are more useful for predicting affective than job production outcomes. This means that interest or affinity for a job rather than the capability to perform can be reliably assessed in an interview. As we know that interest and affinity are related to job satisfaction, commitment, absenteeism, and turnover, interviews are clearly potentially useful predictors of these participation outcomes, but not of productivity (Crites, 1969; Mowday, Porter and Steers, 1982; Schmitt, 1976).

Some evidence for the usefulness of interviews as predictors of turnover comes from the research on the Realistic Job Preview (RJP; Wanous, 1980). The RJP is based on the principle that the selection process is really a two-way process, in which both the individual and the hiring organization obtain useful information. In more than fifteen field experiments it now seems clear that when applicants receive an accurate picture of the job for which they are making application, if hired they are more likely to be satisfied and committed and less likely to become a turnover (Popovich and Wanous, 1982).

Another way of interpreting these data is to say that applicants who come to an interview with more realistic information are more likely to be satisfied, to be committed, and to stay. It seems, then, that the interview would be an excellent opportunity to assess what individuals *do* know and to use that information in a predictive mode. Pulakos and Schmitt (1982), for example, have recently shown that the job satisfaction of young workers on the job for twenty months is as predictable from data collected from them when they were hired regarding their job expectations as it was from actual job satisfaction data collected eleven months after they were hired! These findings and other theoretical issues presented in Schmitt and Schneider (1983) suggest good potential for the use of interviews (or new kinds of data gathering paper and pencil tests; maybe a new kind of work-relevant "personality" test) in predicting important organizational outcomes, although not productivity.

However, industrial practice still appears to be focused on poorly structured interviews used as a basis for predicting productivity at work. This may relate back to the earlier discussion of organizations not being clear about their goals and then thus failing to understand the full range of what effectiveness means. Few companies, for example, maintain useful turnover data. If they have it at all, the data will only be of the most gross percentage sort—55 percent turnover. Where the turnover is, and who is becoming a turnover, are rarely tracked. Indeed, the idea that one can predict turnover, indeed predict job satisfaction, would probably come as a surprise to most managers and some I/O Psychologists (Schmitt & Schneider, 1983; Schneider, 1976).

Exercises. Better predictors of productivity kinds of behaviors are exercises—opportunities for applicants to display (or at least report on) job-relevant behavior. There really is a continuum of behavioral exercises that underlies the personnel selection model for predicting productivity behavior, from

Paper and pencil tests
↓
Situational interviews
↓
Simulations

A paper and pencil test is an exercise that is typically quite removed from the actual behavior required by a job. However, situational interviews (for instance, Latham, Saari, and Purcell, 1980) put the applicant psychologically in the kinds of behavior-requirement situations they will encounter at work and ask them to say what they would actually do. Simulations (or work samples) are actual pieces of the job. One would expect that the validity of these different kinds of exercises would improve, the more like the actual job the exercise is, but to my knowledge little research exists on this issue (but see Gordon and Kleiman, 1976 for one such study). What is clear is that simulations or work samples are consistent predictors of work performance (Asher and Sciarrino, 1976).

In fact, an interesting technique called the Biographical Information Blank (BIB) is a strategy for assessing samples of how people have behaved *in the past*. BIBs are known to be excellent predictors when developed following the selection validation model (Owens, 1976). In brief, the literature on exercises and other samples of behavior (present or past) is impressive and increasingly promising. The best-known example supporting this statement is the Assessment Center (cf. Bray, Campbell, and Grant, 1974; Moses and Byham, 1977); these appear to predict managerial progress and other management criteria with consistent accuracy (Borman, 1982).

The message emanating from this section on selection is that the validation model, when followed, yields useful predictors for different kinds of important outcomes. Some predictors, tests and exercises, seem more useful for predicting production-relevant behaviors while others, especially interviews and/or forms of collecting interest/affinity information, are more likely to be useful against affective/withdrawal criteria.

Utility. Another issue that I/O psychologists have emphasized (Dunnette and Borman, 1979), concerns the utility or cost effectiveness of implementing valid selection procedures. It is clear, however, that degree of validity is only one consideration in whether to adopt a particular selection procedure. For example, a paper and pencil test costing $5.00 per applcant with validity of .30 has more utility than an interview costing $50.00 per applicant with validity of .35 when the job is one where there are many applicants and the current work force is not very satisfactory. Conversely, when the job is very important for overall organizational effectiveness and when there are few applicants and an error is very costly, recruitment and selection costs become less relevant and validity determines the decision. In brief, then, the utility issue involves a comparison of the costs of making an error against the costs of gathering the data to be used as a basis for making a decision. This comparison is conditional on the number of available applicants, the current state of the workforce (how good or bad it is now), and the validity of the proposed procedure.

The details of utility analysis have been worked out by Cronbach and Gleser (1965) but, as is obvious from this brief outline, the procedure requires the maintenance of relatively complete and certainly accurate human resources records, something few companies seem willing to do. This failure will prove particularly unfortunate now that the business world is moving increasingly into information and service and the corporation's capital asset will be its human resources. It is interesting, then, that companies maintain accurate records on equipment and machinery purchases and maintenance and are willing to create task forces to make capital expenditures of $250,000. However, to hire an employee whose salary alone in 10 or fewer years will cost them that much, they fail to invest in validating their selection procedures unless ordered by a court and they fail to keep data on employee "maintenance." The paradox in this will become clearer in the very near future because our corporate, and perhaps societal, welfare may well partially depend on the appropriate match of people to jobs (Hunter and Schmidt, 1982) and the retention of quality people.

The reader should not assume from this glowing support of the selection validation model that all is well, just that a lot is known and that the technology works. As Schmitt and Schneider (1983) have noted, there is much work still to be done in fully understanding the role of job analysis in selection; the implications of the Schmidt and Hunter validity generalization findings and their arguments about utility; the lack of attention paid to the prediction of affectively-tinged criteria (satisfaction, absenteeism, turnover); a general failure of selection researchers to address the contribution of selection to organizational effectiveness; and the use of non-ability predictors of important work behaviors and outcomes. But Schmitt and Schneider (1983) were looking to where else we can go, and they clearly are impressed with the contributions made by, and the future potential of, personnel selection.

Training

Evaluation Models

In the history of the I/O field, training research and an emphasis on the validity of training came after the selection validation model was well understood (Glaser, 1982; Goldstein, 1974; McGehee and Thayer, 1961). In fact, while the experimental and quasi-experimental designs for validating experiments in natural setting summarized and popularized by Campbell and Stanley (1963) were viewed by most applied behavioral scientists as a major breakthrough, selection researchers viewed such models as mere extensions of the selection validation model.

The contemporary training research literature is dominated by a validation model that is conceptually very similar to the selection model. The major difference is that the typical training research design emphasizes relative changes in, and performance of, groups rather than correlations between individual attributes and individual performance. Thus, the aims of any training program are to change those who are trained and to show that those who are changed are more likely to meet established criteria than those who are not trained. If one thinks about those who are changed in a training program as high scorers on a test and those not trained as low scorers, then the analogy to the test validation model is quite clear.

A typical training validation (or "evaluation") program would have the following sequence:

1. Needs analysis: a more complex form of job analysis involving not only what behaviors the job requires but an assessment of where the *organization* most needs training and the contextual conditions that may inhibit transfer from training to the job ("organization analysis") and which persons currently in the organization need what kinds of training ("person analysis") so they can meet job requirements.
2. Development of criteria; as will be noted later, training researchers have been very concerned about criteria and have contributed

some conceptual schemes that help differentiate among criteria of different kinds.

3. Development of a training program; a considerable variety of methods exists in training, just as there are numerous kinds of predictors. Some methods will be briefly discussed.
4. Validation ("evaluation") of the training program; there has been a tendency for training programs to go unvalidated, especially when the people responsible for them are unsophisticated with respect to evaluation.
5. Utility analysis.

As the reader can see, a training development and evaluation program will follow a similar sequence to the selection validation model.

With respect to criteria, Kirkpatrick (1959) defined four types of criteria that could be used as a basis for evaluating training programs:

1. Reaction criteria—what did the trainees think of the experience?
2. Learning criteria—did the trainees make some progress compared to non-trainees? at the end of the training had there been changes?
3. Behavior criteria—do trainees behave more appropriately on the job than non-trainees? does the training "transfer" from the class to the job?
4. Results criteria—what were earlier called output criteria. Were there changes in job proficiency or promotability noticed when comparing trainees to non-trainees?

As Campbell (1971) showed, there has been an unfortunate emphasis, by non-I/O psychologists, on Kirkpatrick's reaction criteria, frequently of the personal testimony sort. Most people responsible for running training programs just have not received sufficient indoctrination in methodology to realize that what looks and feels good may not be valid regarding behavioral and results criteria. Indeed, early attacks on fads adopted by business such as T-Groups (Dunnette and Campbell, 1968) focused on the paucity of appropriate research designs for evaluating their effectiveness. Perhaps these kinds of attacks resulted in the more appropriate kinds of validity studies reported by Smith (1975) showing that T-Groups in fact had some positive validity also for learning, behavior, and results criteria.

Increasingly, some sophistication is entering the validation of training programs, pushed perhaps by the development and application of appropriate evaluation strategies (cf. Cook and Campbell, 1979). These strategies, developed primarily in the public policy anbd education fields, have illuminated a large number of the methodological pitfalls constraining the researcher who tries to draw conclusions about the relative effectiveness of *any* intervention, including training.

Campbell (1971), Goldstein (1974, 1978), and Wexley and Latham (1981), in particular, have championed the application of these designs to evaluating training programs. They have put an unyielding emphasis on needs analysis as the foundation of any effort and the requirement that transfer of training (results criteria) be demonstrated. Indeed, Goldstein (1978) has even argued that training researchers should attempt to demonstrate a kind of validity generalization (what he called "interorganizational validity") for their programs; that is, that a training program developed in one setting will be effective across a number of different settings. Some of the kinds of data necessary to establish this interorganizational validity are now beginning to be accumulated.

These data can accumulate because of the very broad variety of types of training programs that exist and the wide variety of criteria against which they are used. Thus, from computer-assisted knowledge acquisition for programmers to behavior modeling for supervisors and from teaching the hard-core unemployed how to find a job to helping alleviate obsolescence in engineers, training is big business, and the potential for conducting meta-analysis or validity generalization studies will increase.

Examples of Training that Work

Some recent progress has been made in accumulating data for meta-analysis, particularly in the area of supervisory training following the behavioral modeling approach proposed by Goldstein and Sorcher (1974). This approach, based on Bandura's (1971) social learning model, capitalizes on the idea that the imitation of social models is an important component of an individual's behavior. Behavioral modeling presents trainees with videotapes of people handling supervisory problems (for instance, poor work quality, excessive absenteeism) in appropriate ways and encourages trainees to model literally what they have seen. Through practice and feedback (two well-known principles of learning), quite dramatic changes in the behavior of supervisors towards subordinates have been observed from pilot efforts in a number of corporate settings, such as GE (Burnaska, 1976), IBM (Kraut, 1976), and AT&T (Moses and Ritchie, 1976); at Weyerhauser similar results were obtained from a "real-time" effort (Latham and Saari, 1979).

Another training program that seems to yield consistent positive results builds on the behavior modification theory of Skinner (for example, 1969). This theory suggests that desired behaviors can be maintained if they are reinforced (rewarded) once they are emitted. The critical features of behavior modification are (1) explicit knowledge of the behaviors that are desired so they can be reinforced and (2) explicit knowledge of undesired behaviors so they will never be reinforced (and thus be extinguished). Because the behavior modification approach is so clear about the necessity for specifying the criterion behaviors of interest it helps illuminate the critical role of needs analysis in training.

There is no doubt that training programs that include reinforcement work but there is some argument over whether reinforcement alone (especially in the absence of goals) works. However, without getting too wrapped up in this theoretical discussion, in companies as diverse as lumbering (Latham and Kinne, 1974) and bakeries (Komacki, Barwick, and Scott, 1978), and with criteria as different as truck load capacity and safety, respectively, approaches like behavior modification seem to work.

These two examples of the accumulation of data supporting validity generalization of a training procedure are encouraging. However, still to be answered for training in business and industry are questions such as which kinds of training should be used to achieve which kinds of criteria for which kinds of trainees. For example, Fiedler (cf. Fiedler and Mahar, 1981) employed programmed instruction, not behavioral modeling, to teach leadership, and Locke and colleagues (cf. Locke, Shaw, Saari, and Latham, 1981) use goal setting to achieve results similar to those obtained with behavior modification. In education, much work on this kind of issue already exists (Goldstein, 1980) and some hypotheses for business and industrial applications await testing (Gagne and Briggs, 1981; Wexley and Latham, 1981).

In addition, debate still exists about the relevance of principles of learning derived from laboratory learning experiments for training programs in business and industry. Of the various principles, practice, feedback and reinforcement seem most useful while distinctions between massed and distributed learning and whole versus part learning appear less germane (Wexley and Latham, 1981). Recently, some newer conceptualizations of the issues involved in skill and knowledge acquisition both at work and in educational settings seem to offer some help for the design of training programs and training program environments. These developments (cf. Gagne and Briggs, 1981) leave the laboratory learning experiment to the students of memory and cognition. The laboratory is replaced with the language of the criterion behaviors required for effective performance and a deep concern for transfer of training to the job and its context (Goldstein, 1980).

Finally, only in the past ten years or so has enough attention been paid to the actual validation of training programs. As noted earlier, for unknown reasons training programs have not received the same attention by I/O psychologists as have selection programs. Indeed, only since the work of Campbell and Stanley (1962) describing validity strategies, McGehee and Thayer's (1961) systematic approach to training, and the review of the training literature by Campbell (1971) has the validation of training become anything like an ordinary event. By the early 1960s, in contrast, selection validation was a well-practiced and well-understood process with a voluminous literature. It is clear that without validity studies, the utility of training programs cannot be known. There is much to be learned still about the development and evaluation of training but, as with selection, when the training evaluation model is followed, it produces productive employees.

Work Motivation

In I/O, the 1940s and 1950s might be called the peak years of emphasis on new applications of personnel selection and the 1970s a time of progress in training research. These two aspects of the field may be labelled personnel-oriented, in the sense that they deal with the entry of individuals into the work setting including what they bring to the setting and how they are changed so they can do their jobs. The 1960s and 1970s were the age of organizational psychology and, within that, work motivation and job satisfaction.

Central to the 1960s and 1970s emphasis on these post-entry issues was a seemingly fortuitous string of important theoretical works bounded approximately by Argyris (1957) and Vroom (1964), with Herzberg, Mausner and Snyderman (1959), McGregor (1960), and Likert (1961) in between. What these works had in common was the idea that the motivation of workers was the result of an interaction between the nature of people and the work situation they encountered; that motivation was not something one can observe in the absence of eliciting stimuli. Of course, the theories differed in the identification of these stimuli but, from a very practical standpoint, they said to management: "Look, your workers have the motivation to do their jobs well if you'd only provide them the right reasons to reveal their motivation." Lack of motivation, then, changed from something to blame on the worker to something to blame on management policy, including managerial philosophy.

The management philosophy required by the theories was twofold: that people have desired they wish to have satisfied by working; and that these desires include, but extend beyond, money (Whyte, 1955, Lawler, 1981). The first issue, that workers have desires, required management to acknowledge that workers were human. The second issue, that workers desire money and other outcomes, required management to acknowledge the complexity of their human resources (Schein, 1965).

And what was management to gain from adopting these perspectives on the *Human Side of Enterprise* (McGregor, 1960)? They were to gain a workforce that contributed their initiative and talent to organizational goal accomplishment, that was committed to organizational goals and objectives, that was experiencing improved feelings of self worth and job satisfaction, and that was more likely to attend work and less likely to turn over.

Note that the effectiveness criteria specified above took an interesting conceptual shift from speaking about individual behavior to work force behavior, that is, a subtle shift took place from the level of the individual to the level of the firm.[2] By this shift, the theoreticians were able to move outside the individual to the organization's policies and practices as a source of explanation for "poor motivation."[3]

All these theoreticians were concerned with helping organizations grow and develop through a focus on the nature of people. Except for Vroom (1964), though, these commentators tended to describe people in more universalistic terms rather than in the individual differences mode so characteristic of personnel selection. For this reason, somewhat of a split in I/O developed between the selection researchers and the more organizationally oriented motivation researchers and, to a great extent, they have gone their separate ways. The latter groups in particular was instrumental in the founding of the field of organizational behavior. Only recently, in writings by such people as Beer (1980) and Schneider (1983), has a rapprochement between the two been suggested.

Vroom's Expectancy Formulation

Vroom's perspective did fall in the middle ground, emphasizing both the nature of man and individual differences, and his perspective dominated the study of motivation by I/O researchers for about ten years. His perspective was actually a pulling together of various theories of learning from basic psychology (for instance, Tolman, 1959) and the field theory of Lewin (for instance, Lewin, 1951). Quite rational in form, the theory postulated that people will behave in ways that they perceive they are able to and that they believe will be instrumental in the attainment of desirable outcomes. Level of performance differences between people, then, were attributed to differences in one, two, or three cognitions: differences in what people desired, differences in beliefs about which levels of performance were necessary to obtain desired outcomes, and/or differences in perceptions of the ability to behave in the way necessary for the attainment of outcomes.

Literally thousands of studies were conducted on one or more versions of this Valence–Instrumentality–Expectancy (VIE) Theory (for a review, see Campbell and Pritchard, 1976). Generally speaking, this literature suggests, as Vroom originally proposed, that point predictions of individual differences in levels of productivity are not particularly accurate but predictions of discrete choices (choice of one job over another, decision to turnover) can be valid. In addition, the evidence indicates that differences in the desirability (valence) of outcomes is not as important as are differences in perceptions of ability to engage in behavior (expectancy) and beliefs about the behaviors that will yield desired outcomes (instrumentality). As a result of these conclusions, by the middle to late 1970s, Vroom's VIE theory was no longer receiving as much attention, the focus having shifted to a more organizationl and job design focus on the one hand and the goal-setting paradigm on the other.

I/O psychologists were probably attracted to VIE theory because of its inclusion of individual differences in desires and its foundation in the more basic psychologies of learning and motivation. Thus, although Vroom (1964) presented his formulation somewhat later than Argyris (1957), Herzberg et al. (1959), Likert (1961), and McGregor (1960), these latter perspectives on motivation would prove quite resistant to immediate attempts at validation. These perspectives required the development of measures of *organizational* and *job* attributes and I/O Psychologists were not accustomed to dealing with assessing features of the context in which people worked as sources of influence on their behavior.

Organization and Job Redesign

I/O psychologists did try to work at the job and organizational levels of analyses. Probably pushed by business and industry's adoption of many of McGregor's and Argyris' ideas, I/O researchers began attempts to understand the role of context as a motivator of behavior. Especially at the University of Michigan, an intensive focus on the development of organizational diagnosis strategies resulted in a set of theories, procedures, and measures that would have considerable influence on what organizational psychologists and behaviorists did and how they conceptualized their role. The theoretical perspectives (for example, Katz and Kahn, 1966, 1978) placed individuals in organizational contexts and organizations in their environmental context in a sort of nested set, each interacting with, and affecting, the other in an open system. Katz and Kahn shoved I/O the final step into a more complete understanding of the role of organizational and job variables in understanding behavior. I think that the Argyrises and McGregors had primed a group of organizational psychologists to look beyond selection and individual differences to the functioning organization as a source for important correlates of behavior and that they were then ready for Katz and Kahn's inclusion of the larger environment.

Perhaps of equal importance to the theoretical breakthroughs were the procedural and methodological developments. In brief, the Michigan researchers evolved strategies for entering organizations, convincing them to employ diagnostic strategies, and showing them how to change (cf. Bowers, 1973). Central to this very programmatic effort was the evolution of sets of measures for diagnosing organizational functioning and the use of those measures as one way of validating intervention and change efforts. The Michigan approach (cf. Nadler, 1977) has evolved into one such comprehensive set of measures—and now there are others (see Lawler, Nadler, and Cammann, 1980; Van de Ven and Joyce, 1981).

At a more immediately individual level, at the same time the organizational diagnosis and assessment efforts were becoming a major force in I/O, job design as a source of employee motivation received research attention. Herzberg et al. (1959) have been given primary credit for promoting job design as a source of employee motivation (Steers and Porter, 1979). Indeed, a series of experiments at AT&T, based on the Herzberg theory of enriching and enlarging jobs, proved very effective in terms of increased productivity and attitudes for clericals (Ford, 1969). This, combined with the availability of a theory resulted in a program of research by Hackman and colleagues (cf. Hackman and Oldham, 1980) into the nature of the psychology of tasks. Their efforts, too, have yielded a set of diagnosis and assessment tools (the Job Diagnostic Survey or JDS) that appears useful also for validation efforts when job redesign is attempted.

Mainstream I/O psychologists by and large have not become as involved in organizational diagnosis and change nor job redesign as they have in personnel selection, training, and tests of variants of VIE and goal setting theory. This is probably because I/O psychologists seem more comfortable with individually relevant criterion behaviors, and when they have attempted validation of organizational interventions, little in the way of individual changes in productivity emerges. So from a strict individual productivity standpoint, I/O psychologists would probably abandon these more macro approaches in favor of an intervention that has a rapid impact on the kinds of individual criterion behaviors that can be reliably assessed. As will be discussed later, some confusion over which theoretical perspectives require testing at which levels of data analysis (individual, group, or organization) has resulted in inappropriate tests of different theories. For example, McGregor's concepts probably require multiple settings, not many individuals in one setting, for exploring the validity of the conceptualization.

Goal-Setting and Organizational Behavior Modification

Two recent approaches to productivity at work, goal-setting (cf. Locke, Shaw, Saari, and Latham, 1981) and behavior modification (cf. Luthans and Kreitner, 1975), both depend on very clear specification of individual behavior as criteria for evaluation purposes, so I/O psychologists seem to feel more at home with these theories. Goal-setting, in particular, seems generalizable to many kinds of jobs from loading logging trucks (Latham and Baldes, 1975) to the effectiveness of scientists and engineers (Latham and Mitchell, 1976). By focusing on individuals and by carefully specifying the criteria of interest in behavioral terms, Locke and his colleagues (cf. Locke et al., 1981) have repeatedly shown that people who have or are assigned difficult, specific goals and who receive feedback on their performance will outperform people who have easy, "do your best" goals and/or who do not receive feedback. The results from various goal-setting studies against specific behavioral criteria have been so effective that an entire performance appraisal system has evolved around this approach to productivity (Latham and Wexley, 1981).

Another recent development in promoting worker productivity that builds on a careful specification of the behaviors of interest is called Organizational Behavior Modification, or O.B. Mod. This is an application of Skinnerian or operant conditioning to the behavior of individual employees emphasizing the importance of reinforcements when appropriate behavior is observed. Luthans and Kreitner (1975), indeed, have proposed an entire framework for organizational change that is based on O.B. Mod.

From an organizational effectiveness perspective these findings are open to various interpretations. Argyris (1976, 1980), for example, might suggest that a concern for the minute specification of individual behavioral outcomes allows rigor of the research design to overwhelm the potential for creating vigor in the organization. Or, Katz and Kahn (1978) would note that O.B. Mod ignores both the organization as a social system and the individual as an intentional, decision-making, self-controlled organism. Both Argyris and Katz and Kahn would argue, then, that long-term consequences for some kind of ultimate organizational effectiveness are being sacrificed for short-run individually oriented boosts in productivity.

The Individual or the Organization:
Horns of a Dilemma

In fact we are somewhat on the horns of a dilemma in that both immediate productivity gains and long-term effectiveness are required in organizations. One potential avenue of escape is to begin conducting evaluations of productivity improvement attempts concurrently at *both* the individual and the organizational level. For example, the performance appraisal approach to productivity outlined by Latham and Wexley (1981) reveals that individuals who are appraised using their behaviorally based procedures are more productive than those who are appraised in the usual manner. Such findings indicate the validity of their approach at the individual level. At the organizational level one needs to ask questions such as (1) is the organization somehow improved (has there been an increase in market shares?; are there more patents now than there were before?); and (2) has the organization improved its relative position vis-à-vis important competitors (is repeat business better than the competition?; how are turnover rates compared to the competition?; and, when possible, what is productivity like compared to the competition?). Models for these kinds of individual and organizational level evaluations now exist (Cook and Campbell, 1979) and they need to be employed—as noted earlier, for evaluating all kinds of I/O interventions, including selection, training, performance appraisal, and motivation.

The idea that all kinds of human resources interventions require both individually and organizationally based evaluations suggests another universal admonition—attempts at having an impact on productivity and other important outcomes (scrappage, accidents, absenteeism, turnover) through motivation strategies need to be evaluated for their utility. Thus, while personnel selection programs quite frequently include utility estimates, and training program evaluations sometimes provide data on utility, motivation improvement programs almost never include any estimates regarding utility (Dunnette, 1982). The formulae provided by Cronbach and Gleser (1965), and discussed briefly earlier, are relevant for estimating utility for any organizational intervention.

Sometimes called behavioral, or human resources accounting, only

Likert (See Likert and Bowers, 1969) and a few others (for instance, Flamholtz, 1974) have championed conversion of non-selection validity data into dollars. However, when this conversion is done, some astonishing figures emerge for even marginal correlations between the intervention and various organizationally relevant outcomes. This should not be so surprising when one considers, say, the costs of an error in a nuclear power plant, or a commercial jet airliner, or a space shuttle. The point here is that, as Dunnette (1982) noted, I/O psychologists have been perhaps ultra-conservative in recommending change precisely because they have tended to ignore utility or behavioral accounting issues. In breif, when conversions to dollars are made, and dollars are the language of management, the utility of even moderate validity is frequently quite remarkable (Hunter and Schmidt, 1982).

Job Satisfaction

For about thirty years (Brayfield and Crockett, 1955), it has been clear that the relationship between individual satisfaction and individual productivity converges around zero. And for longer than that it has been theoretically clear that motivation refers to the activation and direction of behavior that resulted in satiation. Still, researchers try to relate various measures of satisfaction to productivity.

Satisfaction and other attitudes regarding work and the work setting are related to organizational effectiveness because dissatisfied workers tend to be absent, tend to turn over, tend to be uncommitted to larger organizational goals and values, and tend to be less cooperative (cf. Mowday, Porter and Steers, 1981). From a utility standpoint, then, satisfaction is an important variable to study.

I/O psychologists have certainly studied it! Locke (1976) reported that some 3300 articles or dissertations existed; the number is probably double that now. Fifty years of study and theories (since the Hawthorne studies of the 1930s) suggest the following conclusions:

1. Confusion exists over what is a theory of work motivation and what is a theory of job satisfaction. Contributing to this confusion have been the theories of worker motivation that are universalistic in tone and/or that relate more to organizational functioning, for instance, McGregor (1960) and Herzberg et al. (1959). These theories, generalizing from personality formulations of the Maslow (1954) sort, specify the kinds of management philosophy and job design that encourage a superior quality of work life through job satisfaction and improved feelings of self worth. In addition, they postulate improved *organizational* functioning; they say little about how an individual's satisfaction

will be reflected in that individual's productivity. In other words, just about all tests of the relationship between individual satisfaction and individual performance in an organization fail to test adequately the organizational functioning hypothesis.

As with the previous topics discussed, then, a failure to evaluate both the individual and the organizational correlates of the issue of interest (selection, training, motivation, satisfaction) may have resulted in an invalid judgment about an hypothesized relationship. From the perspective of Roberts, Hulin and Rousseau (1979), conceptualization of these problems has not been precise regarding the individual or aggregate level of analysis for research.

The more macro or universalistic formulations about work motivation imply things about what will satisfy *all* (or just about all) workers. They are motivation theories in the sense that they make assumptions about what people in general want, need or desire and that they will be more rather than less satisfied upon attainment of those desires. Those theories say nothing about how much effort (activation) people will put forth in pursuit of attainment, nor which kinds of behavior (direction) they are likely to display. In that sense, they are really more theories of satisfaction than of motivation.

2. Certain organizational events, agents and conditions appear to lead to worker satisfaction (Locke, 1976):

Mentally challenging and physically undemanding work.

Equitable rewards (of all kinds including pay and promotion) tied to performance.

Supervisors and colleagues who facilitate reward attainment, who are competent, and friendly/supportive.

Company policies that promote reward attainment and that are relatively unambiguous and nonconflictual.

These more or less universal satisfiers seem relatively unaffected by people's characteristics such as race, sex, or age (Weaver, 1977).

3. The assessment of job satisfaction is a can of worms. Because no common, shared, theory of job satisfaction exists, various researchers adopt their own focus and their own measures. Apparently agreement fails to exist even about whether satisfaction is an *evaluation* of events, agents, and conditions or beliefs/descriptions about their *existence*. So, even at the most fundamental level, some still argue whether assessment of such conditions as equitable rewards tied to performance are really just the same as measuring job satisfaction. The answer, of

course, is that some conditions, like the one noted, are universally satisfying, so similar findings emerge from beliefs about them and evaluations of them. However, regarding such issues as the extent to which workers are reinforced for wearing ear plugs (Zohar, 1980), or whether managers meet with subordinates to plan new campaigns to give good customer service (Schneider, 1980), no such universals appear to exist, and the condition is assessable independently of the evaluation of it (Schneider, 1975).

A measure of job satisfaction that seems to be cognizant of this kind of thinking and that has received considerable research support is the Job Descriptive Index (JDI) of Smith, Kendall and Hulin (1969). It was designed around an evaluation/comparison model of job satisfaction supplemented by considerable inductive theory. It is a facet measure of satisfaction, tapping the work itself, pay, opportunities for promotion, supervision and co-workers.

Many of the items on the JDI (there are 72 items, 18 each for the work itself, supervision, and coworkers and 9 for the others) are on the "universal satisfier" end of the description continuum (challenging work, considerate supervision, pay for performance) and others are more clearly evaluative (satisfying work). The measure is quite easily administered, yields easily interpretable data because of the availability of national norms to use as a basis for comparison, has only moderate facet intercorrelations (less than .40) and correlates well with numerous other measures of satisfaction.

Researchers not happy with the JDI may be interested in a book by Cook, Hepworth, Wall, and Warr (1981) that exhaustively reviews and presents 294 job attitude measures. Given the availability of the JDI, however, unless the reader is testing some new facet of job satisfaction I urge him or her to use the JDI; if not the JDI then some well-evaluated measure in Cook et al. (1981). As Landy and Trumbo (1980, p. 415) put it: "we *beg* you not to develop another scale."

This should not be interpreted to mean that the JDI or other evaluation-oriented measures are useful diagnostic procedures, because they may not be. Diagnoses should yield specification of critical agents, events and conditions; those that lead to dissatisfaction and/or ineffective individual or organizational performance. For example, what makes a job "challenging", or a supervisor "impolite," or coworkers "lazy"? In a sense, then, job satisfaction may be viewed as an outcome-oriented performance appraisal, one which focuses on an *evaluation* of what has happened rather than *how*. It is difficult to translate such appraisals into, for example, training programs to improve performance outcomes. Similarly, job satisfaction measures will typically be outcome-oriented rather than focusing in on the specific events, agents or conditions that can be altered to improve satisfaction. In this light, the interested reader will find Beer's (1980) discussion of organizational diagnosis to be informative and the Cook et al. (1981) useful.

4. Some individual outcomes of importance to organizational effectiveness, although not to direct measures of productivity, are related to job satisfaction. The most consistent correlate of job satisfaction is employee turnover, and this relationship has been documented frequently (see Mobley, 1982 for a review). Absenteeism is less clearly related to satisfaction, except apparently when people must make a real choice about whether or not to be absent. In an innovative test of this hypothesis Smith (1977) showed that unit attitude data correlated strongly with unit absenteeism during a blizzard but not under typical weather conditions. Work quality, employee wellness, smoothness of organizational functioning, safety and lack of waste tend to also be positively related to job satisfaction (Katz and Kahn, 1978). And, both theoretically (Thompson, 1967) and empirically (Schneider, Parkington, and Buxton, 1980), employee satisfaction in service organizations is positively related to consumer satisfaction.

Listing of these correlates of job satisfaction is meant to indicate why I/O psychologists continue to study the phenomenon. Indeed it seems clear to this author that while no meaningful relationship between individual satisfaction and individual productivity may exist, the relationship between an *aggregate* of employees and various *aggregate* outcomes can be clearly demonstrated (Beer, 1980; Katz and Kahn, 1978). Unfortunately, few direct utility analyses of the importance of job satisfaction have been reported; these need to be accomplished before the role of employee evaluations of their organization's performance will become as important as management's evaluation of employee performance (for an exception see Mirvis and Lawler, 1977).

Summary

The two major contributions of I/O Psychology to the study of productivity are concern for the reliable specification and assessment of performance and the clear awareness that worker productivity in terms of output is only one way of indexing worker contributions to organizational effectiveness. In essence, then, I/O psychologists have evolved strategies for assessing the important production-relevant behaviors of people, and they have documented the importance of such other behaviors as turnover and absenteeism to organizations.

Within the confines of the prediction and understanding of individual behavior at work, the I/O personnel selection has been quite effective in making accurate predictions of behavior and outcomes. Using a variety of procedures, from tests to biographical information blanks to job simulations, personnel selection researchers have revealed a consistent capability of producing correlations above .30 between measures taken at time of hire and various subsequent outcomes of interest. The true magnitude of this technological accomplishment is only now being appreciated through calculations of utility. There can no longer be any doubt about the ability to predict on-the-job behavior at the time of hire when the selection validation model is competently followed.

Training models and theories of work motivation also appear useful as predictors of individual behavior. Indeed, frequently training has focused on teaching motivation theory to managers! So, for example, O.B. Mod and goal-setting training are two of the more generalizable training programs, and behavior modeling for supervisors capitalizes greatly on the motivational roles of social support, reinforcement, and feedback as vehicles for changing behavior.

Perhaps the major contribution of I/O to the training literature has been the careful documentation of the idea that programs that feel good to participants may have no long-term positive consequences for *either* participants or their employing organization. The consensus in I/O makes it quite clear that training programs, like personnel selection programs, require validation against a broad range of criteria. A second contribution of the training researchers has been a seemingly final break with more laboratory-oriented basic psychological theories and constructs in favor of concepts and techniques that are relevant for the uncontrolled work-a-day world to which training must transfer.

Clearly the foremost contribution of I/O Psychology from a worker motivation vantage point has been the idea that all workers are motivated; the question is how organizations can be managed to activate and direct that motivation towards organizationally relevant behaviors and outcomes. Also of importance has been the development and implementation of organizational diagnostic procedures for identifying events, agents, and conditions that inhibit employee motivation.

Conceptually, the difference between individually focused theories like VIE, goal-setting, and O.B. Mod and the more macro or universalistic theories like Argyris's or McGregor's has not been explored as much as would seem fruitful. Thus, while it seems clear that I/O can utilize the micro theories to make predictions about individual level behavior, the concepts and methods for making valid predictions about organizational functioning and effectiveness are lacking. Only recently, for example, have more psychologically oriented researchers even entered the organizational effectiveness arena (Campbell, 1977; Steers,

1979) having left this issue to organizational sociologists (cf. Hage, 1980). As has been noted throughout this chapter, I/O Psychologists' ignoring the issue of organizational effectiveness has not been useful and needs to be ended.

Employee satisfaction does appear to be reflected in smoother organizational functioning and less absenteeism, turnover, and accidents and more wellness, cooperation, and employee initiative. There is no evidence that a happy worker produces more widgets per hour, but there is considerable evidence that a company would only have to hire one person per job rather than the 1.2 people per job due to absenteeism.

While some conceptual confusion exists about what motivation is and satisfaction is, the latter seems to have earned its rightful place as a central concern of I/O. This seems to be especially true at the aggregate or unit level where satisfaction ("morale") seems to index something about the social functioning of the unit.

In conclusion, the I/O perspective on productivity offers a broad range of independent variables (predictors) and dependent variables (criteria) in a very loosely coupled system that is increasingly being tied into understandable wholes (Beer, 1980; Katz and Kahn, 1978). This perspective makes it quite clear that a narrow focus on worker productivity narrowly defined will fail to advance our understanding of how organizations grow, function, and decline. The perspective also substantiates the fact that conceptualizing performance of all kinds at both the individual and the unit level may offer additional insights into the reciprocal nature of worker-organization relationships. The present author is betting that, ultimately, it is at the level of worker-organization reciprocity that the action really is (Schneider, 1975, 1976, 1982, 1983).

Notes

1. Irwin L. Goldstein, Susan Jackson, and David Schoorman provided helpful comments on an earlier version of this chapter; I thank them for their help.

2. This was not true for Vroom's perspective.

3. I choose not to discuss Maslow's (1954) perspective because it was through McGregor (1960) that Maslow had his most important impact. However, tests of Maslow's theory on working adults have yielded unimpressive results, most likely because the theory is a developmental theory and because Maslow (and Alderfer, 1972) ad-

dressed the role of desires in satisfaction and not the motivation to produce.

References

Alderfer, C.P. *Existence, relatedness and growth: Human needs in organizational settings.* New York: Free Press, 1972.

Argyris, C. *Personality and organization.* New York: Harper, 1957.

———. Problems and new directions for industrial psychology. In M.D. Dunnette (Ed.), *Handbook of industrial and organizational psychology.* Chicago: Rand McNally, 1976.

———. *Inner contradictions of rigorous research.* New York: Academic Press, 1980.

Arvey, R.D. *Fairness in selecting employees.* Reading, Ma.: Addison–Wesley, 1979.

Bandura, A. *Social learning theory.* New York: General Learning Press, 1971.

Beer, M. *Organization change and development: A systems view.* Santa Monica, Ca.: Goodyear, 1980.

Blum, M.L., and Naylor, J.C. *Industrial psychology: Its theoretical and social foundations.* New York: Harper and Row, 1968.

Boring, E.G. *History of experimental psychology* (2nd ed). New York: Appleton–Century, 1950.

Borman, W.C. Validity of behavioral assessment for predicting military recruiter performance. *Journal of Applied Psychology,* 1982, *67,* 3–9.

Bowers, D.G. OD techniques and their results in 23 organizations: The Michigan ICL study. *Journal of Applied Behavioral Science,* 1973, *9,* 21–43.

Bray, D.W., Campbell, R.J., and Grant, D.L. *Formative years in business: A long-term AT&T study of managerial lives.* New York: Wiley, 1974.

Brayfield, A.H., and Crockett, W.H. Employee attitudes and employee performance. *Psychological Bulletin,* 1955, *52,* 396–424.

Burnaska, R.F. The effects of behavior modelling training upon manager's behavior and employee's perceptions. *Personnel Psychology,* 1976, *29,* 329–335.

Campbell, D.T., and Stanley, J.C. *Experimental and quasi-experimental designs for research.* Chicago: Rand McNally, 1963.

Campbell, J.P. Personnel training and development. In M.R. Rosenzweigh and L.W. Porter (Eds.) *Annual Review of Psychology,* Vol. 22. Palo Alto, Ca.: Annual Reviews, 1971.

————. On the nature of organizational effectiveness. In P.S. Goodman and J.M. Pennings (Eds.), *New perspectives on organizational effectiveness*. San Francisco: Jossey-Bass, 1977.

Campbell, J.P., and Pritchard, R.D. Motivation theory in industrial and organizational psychology. In M.D. Dunnette (Ed.), *Handbook of industrial and organizational psychology*. Chicago: Rand McNally, 1976.

Carlson, R.C., Thayer, P.W., Mayfield, E.C., and Peterson, D.A. Improvements in the selection review. *Personnel Journal,* 1971, *50,* 268–274.

Cook, J.D., Hepworth, S.J., Wall, T.D., and Warr, P.B. *The experience of work.* New York: Academic Press, 1981.

Cook, T.D., and Campbell, D.T. *Quasi-experimentation: Design and analysis issues for field settings.* Chicago: Rand McNally, 1979.

Crites, J.O. *Vocational psychology.* New York: McGraw-Hill, 1969.

Cronbach, L.J., and Gleser, B.C. *Psychological tests and personnel decisions.* Urbana, Ill.: University of Illinois Press, 1965.

Dunnette, M.D. *Human resource utilization and productivity improvement: An integration.* Paper presented at the IAPP Congress, Edinburgh, Scotland, 1982.

Dunnette, M.D., and Borman, W.C. Personnel selection and classification systems. In M.R. Rosenzweigh and L.W. Porter (Eds.) *Annual Review of Psychology,* Vol. 30. Palo Alto: Annual Reviews, 1979.

Dunnette, M.D., and Campbell, J.P. Laboratory education: Impact on people and organizations. *Industrial Relations,* 1968, *8,* 1–27.

Fiedler, F.E., and Mahar, L. The effectiveness of contingency model training: A review of the validation of leader match. *Personnel Psychology,* 1979, *32,* 45–62.

Fine, S.A. Functional job analysis: An approach to a technology for manpower planning. *Personnel Journal,* 1974, *53,* 813–818.

Fivars, G. The critical incident technique: A bibliography. *Journal Supplement Abstract Service,* 1975, *5,* 210.

Flamholtz, E. Should your organization attempt to value its human resources? *California Management Review,* 1971, *14,* 40–45.

Ford, R.N. *Motivation through the work itself.* New York: American Management Association, Inc., 1969.

Gagne, R., and Briggs, L.J. *Principals of instructional design,* 2nd ed. New York: Holt, Rinehart & Winston, 1981.

Ghiselli, E.E. *The validity of occupational aptitude tests.* New York: Wiley, 1966.

Glaser, R. Instructional psychology: Past, present and future. *American Psychologist,* 1982, *37,* 292–305.

Goldstein, A.P., and Sorcher, M. *Changing supervisory behavior.* New York: Pergamon, 1974.

Goldstein, I.L. *Training: Program development and evaluation.* Belmont, CA: Brooks/Cole, 1974.

———. The pursuit of validity in the evaluation of training programs. *Human Factors,* 1978, *20,* 131–144.

Gordon, M.E., and Kleiman, L.S. The prediction of trainability using a work sample test and aptitude test: A direct comparison. *Personnel Psychology,* 1976, *29,* 243–253.

Guion, R.M. *Personnel testing.* New York: McGraw-Hill, 1965.

Hackman, J.R., and Oldham, G.R. *Work redesign.* Reading, Ma.: Addison-Wesley, 1980.

Hage, J. *Theories of organizations: Form, process, and transformation.* New York: Wiley, 1980.

Herzberg, F., Mausner, B., and Snyderman, B. *The motivation to work.* (2nd ed.) New York: Wiley, 1959.

Hunter, J.E., and Schmidt, F.L. Fitting people to jobs: Implications of personnel selection for national productivity. In E.A. Fleishman (Ed.) *Human performance and productivity.* Hillsdale, NJ: Erlbaum, 1982.

Katz, D., and Kahn, R.L. *The social psychology of organizations.* New York: Wiley, 1966.

———. *The social psychology of organizations* (2nd ed.). New York: Wiley, 1978.

Kirkpatrick, D.L. Techniques for evaluating training programs. *Journal of the American Society of Training Directors,* 1959, *13,* 3–9 and 21–26.

Komacki, J., Barwick, K.D., and Scott, L.R. A behavioral approach to occupational safety: Pinpointing and reinforcing safe performance in a food manufacturing plant. *Journal of Applied Psychology,* 1978, *63,* 434–445.

Kraut, A.I. Developing managerial skills via modeling techniques—some positive research findings: A symposium. *Personnel Psychology.* 1976, *29,* 325–328.

Landy, F.J., and Farr, J.L. Performance rating. *Psychological Bulletin,* 1980, *87,* 72–107.

Landy, F.J., and Trumbo, D.A. *Psychology of work behavior* (rev. ed.). Homewood, Ill.: Dorsey, 1980.

Latham, G.P., and Baldes, J.J. The "practical significance" of Locke's theory of goal setting. *Journal of Applied Psychology,* 1975, *60,* 122–124.

Latham, G.P., and Kinne, S.B. Improving job performance through training in goal setting. *Journal of Applied Psychology,* 1974, *59,* 187–191.

Latham, G.P., and Mitchell, T.R. Behavioral criteria and potential reinforcers for the engineer/scientist in an industrial setting. *JSAS of Selected Documents in Psychology,* 1976, *6,* 38, 1, 316.

Latham, G.P., and Saari, L.M. Application of social learning theory to training supervisors through behavioral modeling. *Journal of Applied Psychology,* 1979, *64,* 239–246.

Latham, G.P., Saari, L.M., Pursell, E.D., and Campion, M.A. The situational interview. *Journal of Applied Psychology,* 1980, *65,* 422–427.

Latham, G.P., and Wexley, K.N. *Increasing productivity through performance appraisal.* Reading, Ma.: Addison-Wesley, 1981.

Lawler, E.E., III. *Pay and organizational development.* Reading, Ma.: Addison-Wesley, 1981.

Lawler, E.E., III., Nadler, D.A., and Camann, C. (Eds.). *Organizational assessment: Perspectives on the measurement of organizational behavior and the quality of work life.* New York: Wiley-Interscience, 1980.

Lewin, K. *Field theory in social science.* Selected theoretical papers edited by D. Cartwright. New York: Harper, 1951.

Likert, R. *New patterns in management.* New York: McGraw-Hill, 1961.

Likert, R., and Bowers, D.G. Organizational theory and human resource accounting. *American Psychologist,* 1969, *24,* 585–592.

Locke, E.A. The nature and causes of job satisfaction. In M.D. Dunnette (Ed.), *Handbook of industrial and organizational psychology.* Chicago: Rand McNally, 1976.

Locke, E.A., Shaw, K.N., Saari, L.M., and Latham, G.P. Goal setting and task performance: 1969–1980. *Psychological Bulletin,* 1981, *90,* 125–152.

Luthans, F., and Kreitner, R. *Organizational behavior modification.* Glenview, Ill.: Scott, Foresman, 1975.

McCormick, E.J. *Job analysis: Methods and applications.* New York: Amacomm, 1979.

McGehee, W., and Thayer, P.W. *Training in business and industry.* New York: Wiley, 1961.

McGregor, D.M. *The human side of enterprise.* New York: McGraw-Hill, 1960.

Maslow, A.H. *Motivation and personality.* New York: Harper, 1954.

Mobley, W.H. *Employee turnover in organizations.* Reading, Ma.: Addison-Wesley, 1982.

Moses, J.L., and Byham, W.C. (Eds.). *Applying the assessment center method.* New York: Pergamon, 1977.

Moses, J.L., and Ritchie, R.J. Supervisory relationships training: A behavioral evaluation of the behavioral modeling program. *Personnel Psychology,* 1976, *29,* 337–343.

Mowday, R.T., Porter, L.W., and Steers, R.M. *Employee-organizational linkages: The psychology of committment, absenteeism, and turnover.* New York: Academic Press, 1982.

Nadler, D.A. *Feedback and organizational development: Using data-based methods.* Reading, Ma.: Addison-Wesley, 1977.

Owens, W.A. Background data. In M.D. Dunnette (Ed.) *Handbook of industrial and organizational psychology.* Chicago: Rand McNally, 1976.

Popovich, P., and Wanous, J.P. The realistic job preview as persuasive communication. *Academy of Management Review,* 1982, *7,* 570–578.

Pulakos, E., and Schmitt, N. *Prediction of job satisfaction: An exploration of expectations.* Unpublished manuscript, Department of Psychology, Michigan State University, 1982.

Roberts, K.H., Hulin, C.L., and Rousseau, D.M. *Developing an interdisciplinary science of organizations.* San Francisco: Jossey-Bass, 1978.

Schein, E.H. *Organization/Psychology.* Englewood Cliffs, N.J.: Prentice-Hall, 1965.

Schmidt, F.L., and Hunter, J.E. Moderator research and the law of small numbers. *Personnel Psychology,* 1978, *31,* 215–232.

———. The future of criterion-related validity. *Personnel Psychology,* 1980, *33,* 41–60.

Schmitt, N. Social and situational determinants of interview decisions: Implications for the employment interview. *Personnel Psychology,* 1976, *29,* 79–101.

Schmitt, N., and Schneider, B. Current issues in personnel selection. In K.M. Rowland and J. Ferris (Eds.) *Research in personnel and human resources management, Vol. 1.* Greenwich, Conn.: JAI Press, 1983.

Schneider, B. Organizational climates: An essay. *Personnel Psychology,* 1975, *28,* 447–479.

———. *Staffing organizations.* Pacific Palisades, Ca.: Goodyear, 1976.

———. The service organization: Climate is crucial. *Organizational Dynamics,* 1980, Autumn, 52–65.

———.Organizational effectiveness: An interactionist perspective. In

D. Whetten and K.S. Cameron (Eds.) *Multiple models of organizational effectiveness.* New York: Academic Press, 1982.

————. Interactional psychology and organizational behavior. In L.L. Cummings and B. Staw (Eds.) *Research in organizational behavior,* Vol. 5. Greenwich, Conn.: JAI Press, 1983.

Sharf, J.C. EEO issues: National Research Council of the National Academy of Sciences Report—*Ability testing: Uses, consequences and controversies. The Industrial-Organizational Psychologist,* 1982, *19,* 34.

Skinner, B.F. *Contingencies of reinforcement: A theoretical analysis.* New York: Appleton-Century-Crofts, 1969.

Smith, F.J. Work attitudes as predictors of attendance on a specific day. *Journal of Applied Psychology,* 1977, *62,* 16–19.

Smith, P.B., Controlled studies of the outcome of sensitivity training. *Psychological Bulletin,* 1975, *82,* 597–622.

Smith, P.C. Behaviors, results, and organizational effectiveness: The problem of criteria. In M.D. Dunnette (Ed.), *Handbook of industrial and organizational psychology.* Chicago: Rand McNally, 1976.

Smith, P.C., Kendall, L.M., and Hulin, C.L. *The measurement of satisfaction in work and retirement: A strategy for the study of attitudes.* Chicago: Rand McNally, 1969.

Steers, R. *Organizational effectiveness: A behavioral view.* Santa Monica, Ca.: Goodyear, 1979.

Steers, R.M., and Porter, L.W. (Eds.) *Motivation and work behavior.* (2nd ed.). New York: McGraw-Hill, 1979.

Tenopyr, M.L. The realities of employment testing. *American Psychologist,* 1981, *36,* 1120–1127.

Thompson, J.D. *Organizations in action.* New York: Wiley, 1967.

Tolman, E.C. Principles of purposive behavior. In S. Koch (Ed.), *Psychology: A study of a science,* Vol. 2. New York: McGraw-Hill, 1959.

Van de Ven, A.H., and Joyce, W.F. (Eds.). *Perspectives on organization design and behavior.* New York: Wiley-Interscience, 1981.

Viteles, M.S. *Industrial psychology.* New York, Norton, 1932.

Vroom, V.R. *Work and motivation.* New York: Wiley, 1964.

Wanous, J.P. *Organizational entry: Recruitment, selection and socialization of newcomers.* Reading, Ma.: Addison-Wesley, 1980.

Weaver, C.N. Relationships among pay, race, sex, occupational prestige, supervision, work, autonomy and job satisfaction in a national sample. *Personnel Psychology,* 1977, *30,* 437–445.

Wexley, K.N., and Latham, G.P. *Developing and training human resources in organizations.* Glenview, Ill.: Scott, Foresman, 1981.

Whyte, W.F. (Ed.) *Money and motivation.* New York: Harper, 1955.

Zohar, D. Safety climate in industrial organizations: Theoretical and applied implications. *Journal of Applied Psychology,* 1980, *65,* 96–102.

8 Personnel Research in Retailing

Arthur P. Brief and
Elizabeth J. Austin

Why does it seem that retailers are expressing increasing concern for such personnel practices as human resources planning, recruitment and selection, training and development, and appraisal and compensation? One obvious response is that top managers in retailing are becoming more aware of the strategic advantage afforded their firms through the acquisition and maintenance of a highly able and motivated labor force.

A question with a not so obvious answer is "Which particular personnel practices are likely to lead to a strategic advantage?" The principle vehicle for supplying answers to this critical question is personnel research. This advocacy of personnel research reflects the belief that as a "way of knowing" (Cohen and Nagel, 1934), personnel research, rooted in the tradition of normal science, provides a substitute for subjectivity. This is the case because personnel researchers, through the methods they employ, aim to produce results that are independently certifiable and not bound by the researcher's opinions or preferences (Hempel, 1965). The competent personnel researcher seeks to collect data in a systematic and controlled manner (Stone, 1978) and to let these data speak for themselves.

In no way should the above advocacy position be interpreted as advancing the position that all personnel research is useful to the retailer; quite the contrary! The intent of this chapter is to outline an agenda of personnel research which would lead to the production of useful knowledge for retailers.

The first section draws a necessary distinction between basic and applied personnel research. Next, the design requirements of useful personnel research are addressed. Third, issues germane to the selection of specific personnel research topics in retailing are articulated. Finally, some general conclusions are drawn that focus on the prospects for the utilization of personnel research results in retailing.

Basic and Applied Personnel Research

One can distinguish between knowledge development and knowledge utilization and the types of research strategies that contribute to each

159

(Kilmann, 1979). Analogously, Kruglanski (1975) identifies two types of research: (a) universalistic or theoretically oriented and (b) particularistic or applied. In the former case, the researcher tentatively claims a universal scope of generality for findings across all sorts and varieties of theoretically irrelevant conditions, with relevancy of a condition determined by the degree to which it is specified in the theory being tested. Most personnel research published in scholarly journals is of the universalistic type. For example, the published research on Vroom's (1964) expectancy theory of work motivations represents attempts to test the theory ignoring such theoretically irrelevant conditions as the types of jobs the subjects of the study perform and the types of organizations in which they are employed. On the other hand, the attention of the researcher doing particularistic or applied research is focused mainly on the accuracy of statements about specific instances, and intended generalizations are restricted in scope. Research aimed at evaluating the impact of a newly implemented compensation system on the performance of the employees of a particular retail outlet is an example of this type of research.

In general, a somewhat arbitrary distinction can be made between basic and applied research (for instance, Cook and Campbell, 1979; Dubin, 1976; Suchman, 1967). Basic research is concerned with the development of knowledge (or theoretical generalizations) through the testing of theory; applied research is concerned with the utilization of knowledge (or the situation-specific utility of particular actions) through the evaluation of complex treatment packages implemented in a precise setting. Kilmann (1979) labels these complex treatment packages as behavioral science technologies. Personnel examples of such technologies include career development programs, assessment centers, sales training programs, and various incentive pay schemes.

Necessarily, the development of personnel knowledge precedes evaluation of its applicability to solving the problems of retailers. Simply, personnel practitioners require behavioral science technologies to apply, and these technologies frequently are suggested by basic personnel research. This is not to say that evaluative research findings cannot contribute to the development of knowledge; indeed, they can (Boehm, 1980). Rather, it is important to recognize the reciprocal relationship between basic and applied research. To the retailer, however, such recognition may be a hard pill to swallow. Retailers are more concerned with solutions than they are with understanding the theoretical reasons why those solutions work (Dubin, 1976). Furthermore, evaluative research findings inherently are more appealing to retailers than basic research findings because evaluative results allow them to ascertain the efficacy of the technologies they have implemented.

Thus, while basic personnel research may not be immediately appealing to retailers, they share a responsibility with other organizational practitioners for encouraging and supporting such research. Again, it is basic research results that likely will supply the technologies that retailers are seeking to apply in order to gain a strategic advantage. Correspondingly, basic personnel researchers are responsible for attempting to communicate their results to retailers. A variety of trade publications (for example, *STORES*) provide likely channels.

Design Requirements for Useful Applied Research

Two of several criteria for evaluation of a research design are internal validity and external validity. Internal validity refers to the degree to which the research design produces results that allow one to make statements about whether there is a causal relationship from one variable to another in the form in which the variables were manipulated or measured; external validity refers to the degree to which the research design produces results that allow one to make statements about the generalizability of the findings (Cook and Campbell, 1979). For example, internal validity concerns how firmly the researcher can state that motivation as measured by Vroom's (1964) formulation, in fact, leads to increased job performance; and external validity concerns how firmly the researcher can state that the observed effects of a compensation program are descriptive of the sample of employees studied or some other sample to which the researcher desires to generalize his or her results.

Since few theories specify crucial target settings, populations, or times to or across which generalization is desired, external validity is relatively unimportant to basic personnel researchers (Berkowitz and Donnerstein, 1982; Cook and Campbell, 1979; Kruglanski, 1975). Conversely, applied personnel researchers and retailers must exhibit high interest in external validity. Retailers, for instance, understandably are interested in knowing what effects, if any, a behavioral science technology produced in the specific sample it was applied to and to what other groups of employees those results might be generalizable.

Most importantly, however, basic and applied personnel researchers as well as retailers should express a dominant concern for internal validity. Obviously, basic researchers principally are interested in the correctness of the theories they are testing. They want to avoid saying that it appears that changes in variable X caused changes in variable Y when, in fact, variables X and Y are causally unrelated. Again, this also should be the dominant concern of applied researchers and retailers. This is the case because considerable costs are associated with being wrong about the magnitude and direction of the effects of an applied behavioral science technology. Assume a retailer concludes that a new compensation program tested one division of his or her firm produced significant increases in sales volume when, in fact, the increases in volume were attributable to some uncontrolled variable like a sharp up-turn in the general economy. Based upon an incorrect conclusion, the retailer goes on to implement the new compensation program throughout all the firm's divisions. In the best of circumstances, the retailer merely would have incurred the costs associated with implementing an ineffectual compensation program; but if the program produced some unintended and negative consequences, such as reduced job satisfaction and consequent increased levels of employee turnover, then the lack of internal validity of the evaluative research design used by the retailer would have yielded exceedingly costly consequences. In sum, applied personnel researchers and retailers should not ignore the importance of external validity nor should they, however, abandon the conventions of rigorous research as advocated by Argyris (1980) and others.

Since retailers can specify the employee populations they want to generalize their evaluative research findings to, random selection of employees or employee groups to be included in the evaluation study is the best means of enhancing external validity (Cook and Campbell, 1979). This implies, at a minimum, that when it is not feasible to investigate the total population of employees, samples be systematically selected and not drawn based upon convenience or some other inappropriate criterion.

With regard to enhancing internal validity, the ideal research design to use is the field experiment, where employees or employee groups are randomly assigned conditions, for example, a control condition and an experimental condition, in which the behavioral science technology to be evaluated is applied. Cook and Campbell (1979) note the resistance of practitioners to support true experiments in their organizations and go on to address a number of alternatives for overcoming such resistance. In reference to the resistance of retailers to the use of true experimental designs, the authors are not aware of one published study in which a field experiment has been conducted in a retail organization. Hopefully, the point has been made, however, that true experimental and other rigorous research designs are in the interest of the retailer. Their use should be predicated on the belief that they will help avoid potentially costly errors in inference.

In total, basic and applied personnel researchers have been urged to rely upon the conventions of rigorous research in retail organizations. Less rigorous and more qualitative and uncontrolled research strategies are unlikely to yield the levels of internal and external validity required. Correspondingly, retailers should not only support the use of rigorous research strategies but also demand them from the researchers, as it is in their own best interest to do so.

Personnel Research Topics in Retailing

In preparing to write this paper, the authors conducted a review of the recently published personnel research in retailing. Publications specifically aimed at retailing audiences as well as more academic journals were searched. In the case of the academic journals (like the *Journal of Applied Psychology* and *Personnel Psychology*), approximately twenty-five articles were isolated for the eight-year period reviewed in which retailing organizations of their employees were the subjects of the study. As anticipated, the research found in these journals was more of the universalistic type rather than being particularistic in nature. Candidly, however, the value of basic research results to retailers, as previously argued, is to suggest behavioral science technologies that can be applied whether or not this basic research was conducted in a retailing organization; therefore, the setting of this research should be of little importance to retailers. For example, a theory of work motivation which has been empirically demonstrated to be plausible in a variety of settings other than retailing could provide retailers with suggestions for formulating specific behavioral science technologies (for instance, a compensation program) to be applied and evaluated in their own organizations.

Regrettably, in the retailing publications reviewed, the research studies found were either also of the universalistic kind or, if particularistic, so poorly designed as to raise serious questions about internal validity. For example, in the *Journal of Retailing* from 1977 through 1981 approximately 20 of more than 125 articles published could be characterized as personnel oriented and, at best, one or two of these report evaluative research findings. In fact, nonempirical pieces on the education of retailers constituted more than half of the personnel-oriented articles found. Of the theoretical papers published most were concerned with the role conflict and ambiguity experienced by retailing personnel (about 4); and, the dependent variable investigated in these studies generally was some measure of job satisfaction, not job performance. While satisfaction clearly is worthy of study in its own right (for example, see Nord, 1977), it seems that retail managers would be more interested in research results which bore directly on job performance and other more tangible outcomes.

Based upon the above discussion, it appears there is a need for the publication of more evaluative research results obtained in retailing organizations and of more universalistic and particularistic results that focus on the performance of retailing personnel. As it stands now, the general body of literature concerned with basic personnel research is of most value to retailing audiences. The breadth and depth of this literature is impressive. One can be confident in asserting that even though most of this literature is not composed of studies conducted in retailing, retailers will find a rich source of results on which to base the behavioral science technologies they are seeking. For example, Schneider (in press) has demonstrated that ample evidence is available to conclude that in the areas of selection, training, and motivation, models and theories exist on which one can base the design of various organizational interventions that will lead to boosts in employee productivity.

But what problems should future personnel research in retailing focus on? This is a difficult question; ultimately, only retailers themselves can supply the answer. In doing so, retailers should specify the conditions they think would exist if those problem were solved. This specificity would assist researchers in identifying the dependent variables of central interest to the retailer and thereby help insure that the research results produced are of use. For instance, the retailer should go beyond stating that he or she has a career development problem and specify the results expected from a successfully functioning career development program (an adequate supply of appropriately trained and motivated employees to be considered for promotions and enhanced job satisfaction; reduced rates of turnover among those employees designated as having managerial talent, and so on).

To reiterate, retailers are best qualified to identify the personnel problems they need solved. Speculating, nevertheless, the most pressing of these problems seem to be concerned with three areas—selection, training, and motivation,[1] to which, according to Schneider (in press), theoretical research is capable of supplying viable options. Selection issues concern the identification of people capable of successfully performing entry-level jobs in sales, buying, and department or store management and people likely to be promoted from these entry positions into the ranks of middle and senior management. Training issues concern the development of people moving into middle and senior management positions. Finally, motivational issues, like selection issues, cut across the functional areas of the retailing organization and concern the motivation to perform as well as the motivation to remain with the organization.

Given the availability of basic knowledge in selection, training, and motivation, the tasks the applied personnel researcher faces are the development and evaluation of retailing-specific behavioral science technologies. While it is beyond the scope of this paper to detail the characteristics of these technologies, an example drawn from the motivation literature will be offered.[2] In a review of all available experimental studies of goal setting, Locke, Feren, McCalek, Shaw, and Denny (1980) found the median improvement in job performance that resulted from goal setting to be 16 percent, and, when goal-setting technologies were combined with monetary incentives, the median improvement in job performance was more than 40 percent. The literature on goal setting and task performance (for instance, Locke, Shaw, Saari, and Lathan, 1981) suggests that the necessary technology merely involves assigning employees specific and challenging goals coupled with a monetary incentive for achieving the assigned goals. In the light of this literature, it seems reasonable to predict that practically significant gains in job performance can be obtained in retailing organizations though implementing the relatively straightforward goal-setting technology described. The evaluative research design would require (a) that the systematic selection of groups of employees (for example, sales departments) be randomly assigned to one of two conditions—an experimental goal-setting condition and a control condition without assigned goals or monetary incentives; (b) for groups assigned to the experimental condition, that specific and challenging goals be formulated and assigned along with the necessary compensation scheme, and (c) that for both experimental and control conditions, pre- and post-experimental measures of job performance (for instance, sales revenues) be collected and analyzed. Assuming that the results of the evaluative study indicate that the goal-setting technology does produce meaningful increases in job performance that outweigh the administrative and other costs associated with the intervention, then the retailer hosting the study could confidently diffuse the technology throughout his or her organization.

The above example, though a simple one, is not unrepresentative of the types of behavioral science technologies that could be developed and evaluated in retailing organizations. Retailers and applied personnel researchers alike need not search out what appears to be the most fashionable and sophisticated in the behavioral sciences. Quite the contrary, they should attempt to apply that knowledge that is time-proven and straightforward and leave the truly new ground to be plowed by the basic researcher.

Conclusion

The intent of this chapter was to outline an agenda for personnel research in retailing. In essence, the agenda suggested called for applied researchers to focus their attentions of the development and evaluation of retailing-specific behavioral science technologies in the areas of selection, training, and motivation. Furthermore, it was urged that these researchers rely upon rigorous methodologies in the conduct of their evaluative studies. In regard to basic personnel research, it was noted that since basic research supplies the framework for required behavioral science technologies and interventions, retailers share a responsibility to support theoretically oriented research efforts even though their results may not be immediately applicable.

Throughout the paper, other potential responsibilities of personnel researchers and retailers were suggested. Two additional ones warrant notice. First, an underlying theme of this paper had been that retailers should demand more of the personnel research community. These demands would require personnel research to address problems of concern to the retailer and not to conduct research which merely is faddish or fashionable in the research community (cf. Dunnette, 1966). In addition, these demands would require personnel researchers to provide the most valid answers possible to the research questions they do address, not to rely on research methods which produce "interesting" but anecdotal evidence. Simply, retailers may view personnel research with disdain because historically they have been satisfied with letting the research community define their personnel problems and to seek solutions to those problems with research techniques of suspect value. Obviously, to make these demands requires retailers to communicate in a precise fashion to personnel researchers the nature of the problems they confront and to become informed as to the appropriateness of alternative research strategies.

Second, personnel researchers are responsible to retailers for not over-advocating the strength of their evaluative research results (Campbell, 1969) or the theoretical base on which various behavioral science technologies are built. In their zeal to service the perceived needs of retailers, some personnel researchers may be tempted to promise more than their data or theory warrant. Retailers should demand a lot from the research community, but demands based upon false expectations can only serve to hurt the cause of both the retailers and the researchers.

Finally, the editors of scholarly and trade publications bear some responsibilities in the research agenda suggested. Namely, they should promote the publication of research results which speak to the efficacy of alternative behavioral science technologies applied in retailing. Beyond evaluating the usefulness of the research results submitted for publication, editors also must attend to the manner in which those results were produced. Even in publications aimed at the trade, it must be the scientific merits of the research which dominates and not the journalistic abilities of the researcher.

In sum, the utilization of personnel research in retailing is seen as increasing only to the extent that retailers, researchers, and journal editors own up to their responsibilities as articulated above. Fulfilling these responsibilities will not be an easy task accomplished overnight; rather, open dialogues among interested parties are a necessary first step. This paper, therefore, is best considered as an initial step in establishing the dialogues required.

Notes

1. The speculations offered are based on a meeting sponsored by New York University's Institute of Retail Management, which was attended by a small group of senior human resource managers in retailing and academic researchers, and on an article by Ornati (1983) on the staffing requirements of department and specialty store chains.

2. For suggestive literature in selection, see, for example, Dunnette and Borman (1979), Schmitt and Schneider (1983); for literature in training, see, for example, Campbell (1971), Goldstein (1974), and Wexley and Latham (1981).

References

Argyris, C. *Inner contradications of rigorous research.* New York: Academic Press, 1980.

Berkowitz, L. and Donnerstein, E. External validity is more than skin deep: Some answers to criticisms of laboratory experiments. *American Psychologist,* 1982, *37*(3), 245–257.

Boehm, V.R. Research in the "Real-World"—A conceptual model. *Personnel Psychology,* 1980, *33,* 494–504.

Campbell, J.P. Personnel training and development. *Annual Review of Psychology,* 1971, *22,* 565–602.

Campbell, J.P. Reforms as experiments. *American Psychologist,* 1969, *24,* 409–429.

Cohen, M. and Nagel, E. *An Introduction to Logic and Scientific Method.* New York: Harcourt, Brace and Co., 1934.

Cook, T.D. and Campbell, D.T. *Quasi Experimentation.* Boston: Houghton Mifflin, 1979.

Dubin, R. Thoery building in applied areas. In M. Dunnette (Ed.)

Handbook of Industrial and Organizational Psychology. Chicago: Rand McNally, 1976.

Dunnette, M. Fads, fashions and folderol in psychology. *American Psychologist,* 1966, *21,* 343–352.

Dunnette, M. and Borman, W.C. Personnel selection and classification systems. *Annual Review of Psychology,* 1979, *30,* 477–525.

Goldstein, I.L. *Training: Program development and evaluation.* Monterey, California: Brooks/Cole Publishing Co., 1974.

Hackman, J.R. and Oldham, G. Development of the job diagnostic survey. *Journal of Applied Psychology,* 1975, *60,* 159–170.

Hempel, C.G. *Aspects of Scientific Explanation,* New York: The Free Press, 1965.

Kilmann, R.H. On integrating knowledge utilization with knowledge development: The philosophy behind the MAPS design technology. *Academy of Management Review,* 1979, *4*(3), 417–427.

Kruglenski, A.W. The human subject in the psychology experiment: Fact and artifact. In L. Berkowitz (Ed.) *Advances in experimental Social Psychology* (vol. 8) New York: Academic Press, 1975.

Lawler, E.E. III Motivation in Work Organizations. Monterey, California: Brooks/Cole Publishing Co., 1973.

Locke, E.A., Fereh, D.B., McCalek, V.M., Shaw, K.N. and Denny, A.T. The effectiveness of four methods of motivating employee performance. In K. Duncan, M. Gruneberg and D. Wallis (Eds) *Changes in Working Life.* New York: Wiley, 1980.

Locke, E.A., Shaw, K.N., Saari, L. and Latham, G.P. Goal setting and task performance: 1969–1981. *Psychological Bulletin,* 1981, *90,* 125–152.

Nord, N.R. Job satisfaction reconsidered. *American Psychologist,* 1977, *32,* 1026–1035.

Ornati, O. Help Wanted! A look at how department and specialty stores plan their manpower changes. *STORES,* January, 1983, 96–100.

Schmitt, N. and Schneider, B. Current issues in personnel selection. In K.M. Rowland and J. Ferris (Eds.), *Research in Personnel and Human Resource Management.* Vol 1, Greenwich, Conn., JAI Press, 1981.

Schneider, B. Industrial and organizational psychology perspective. In A.P. Brief (Ed.) *Productivity Research in the Behavioral and Social Sciences,* New York: Prager, in press.

Stone, E.F. *Research Methods in Organizational Behavior,* Santa Monica, Ca.: Goodyear, 1978.

Suchman, E.A. *Evaluative Research.* New York: Russell Sage, 1967.

Vroom, V. *Work and Motivation.* New York: Wiley, 1964.

Wexley, K.N. and Latham, G.P. *Developing and Training Human Resources in Organizations*. Glenview, Ill.: Scott Foresman and Company, 1981.

About the Contributors

Elizabeth J. Austin is a student at New York University.

Richard Klimoski is a professor of psychology at the Ohio State Univeristy.

Gary P. Latham is a management consultant based in Seattle, Washington.

Edwin A. Locke is a professor of management and psychology at the University of Maryland.

Lise M. Saari is a student in the department of psychology of the University of Washington.

Benjamin Schneider is a professor of psychology at the University of Maryland.

Randall S. Schuler is an associate professor of management at New York University.

Karyll N. Shaw is a student in the College of Business and Management of the University of Maryland.

Kenneth N. Wexley is a professor of management at Michigan State University.

About the Editor

Arthur P. Brief received his Ph.D. from the University of Wisconsin–Madison. He is currently professor of management and organizational behavior at New York University's Graduate School of Business Administration.

Professor Brief has written many articles on organizational behavior and employee motivation. He has also written several books, among them *Productivity Research in the Behavioral and Social Sciences*.